BARRY NORMAN'S VIDEO GUIDE

BARRY NORMAN'S VIDEO GUIDE

Barry Norman and
Emma Norman

A Mandarin Paperback
BARRY NORMAN'S VIDEO GUIDE

First published in Great Britain 1994
by Mandarin Paperbacks
an imprint of Reed Consumer Books Limited
Michelin House, 81 Fulham Road, London SW3 6RB
and Auckland, Melbourne, Singapore and Toronto

Design copyright © 1994 Reed International Books Limited
Text copyright © 1994 Barry Norman, Emma Norman

The authors have asserted their moral rights

A CIP catalogue record for this title
is available from the British Library

ISBN 0 7493 1846 5

Printed and bound in Great Britain
by Cox & Wyman Ltd, Reading, Berks

CONTENTS

INTRODUCTION

Let's begin by making something perfectly clear: you will not find all of these videos in your local store. You will probably not find all of them in a big, specialist store. Some indeed you will not, for a while, find anywhere at all because the films are so recent that they have not been released on video yet. But they will be, sooner rather than later. It's just a question of being patient.

Seeking out videos is a perplexing, irritating business. We know and you know that the titles should be available. All the films listed here – except the very latest ones – have already been issued on video. But where are they? What is really needed is a companion volume, a kind of 'Video Finder's Guide'. If such a thing already exists, then God bless the compilers for they are doing a great public service.

Every week in my office at 'Film 94' I receive a score or more of letters from desperate people asking where they can find a video of such-and-such a film, as if somehow I am privy to a secret source unknown to anyone else. But, alas, I am not. All I can suggest to these unhappy people is that they contact the British Video Association, 21 Poland Street, London, W1, and throw themselves on its mercy. If the BVA doesn't know where or how a video is to be located, either for

hire or for sale, the chances are nobody does.

As for the present book, those of you who saw our 'Good Night in Guide' in 1992 will notice certain differences, but the basic format is much the same. For ease of reference the films are divided into ten loose categories – loose because very few films are simply comedies, or simply dramas, or even simply Westerns. As an added bonus, we have plucked ten choice war movies, mainly from the Action/Adventure section, and added them to our Top Ten lists.

Most importantly, we have restricted our entries to around 1,600 films (there were 1,200 in the 'Good Night in Guide') in the confident belief that when you're out shopping for a video and are not sure which to take you will want a reference book that you can slip into your handbag or your pocket and not some weighty tome that even Arnold Schwarzenegger could hardly lift.

You will not, of course, agree with all our ratings; sometimes, as Emma points out, we didn't agree with each other. But when that happened the more persuasive argument prevailed. Nor will you agree with the choice or placing of the films in our Top Ten lists, but then part of the fun of any such book as this is the passionate discussions it can provoke, among readers as well as compilers. As to those Top Ten lists, incidentally, I should point out that they don't represent our personal favourites among ALL films but merely our favourites among those available on video.

One more thing: may we suggest that you keep this book beside you at all times? After all, it's just as useful for checking out the movies on TV as it is for helping you to choose a video.

Barry Norman

....

THE lovely thing about writing a follow-up to the 'Good Night *in* Guide' was not only the chance to work with my father (which, if I haven't already told him, was great) but to be able to change certain decisions.

Some videos, for instance, have lost a star, others have gained one. The films haven't altered, of course, but our opinions have – invariably as a result of yet another viewing. For example, 'The Freshman' earned another star after we watched it again, whereas 'The Addams Family' lost one in light of the sequel, 'Addams Family Values', which was better.

And there have been one or two changes in our Top Ten lists, though not many. Again, we disagreed on very few decisions, though I never realised Dad could be so stubborn. I was all for dropping 'The Searchers' from the top of the Westerns list and replacing it with 'Butch Cassidy and the Sundance Kid' but he'd have none of it. On the other hand, I dug my heels in and succeeded in upping 'An American Werewolf in London' to second place in the Horror Top Ten, my argument being that it's much underrated and, besides, 'Psycho' looks so dated now.

'Oklahoma!' has found its way into the Best Musicals because we saw it again recently and were struck once more by how very good it is. But only a handful of new films makes it into the lists, reflecting the fact that although some very good movies have come out in the last year or so, there has been very little that is outstanding.

I hope you have as much fun reading this book as we had writing it, and that we can spare you from having to sit through some of the dire films we have had to suffer.

Happy viewing.

Emma Norman

TOP TENS

These are our recommendations for ten special videos in each genre which should be readily available, or at least easily obtainable, by your local store. There are of course many other great films we would have liked to include, but for one reason or another they are sadly less easy to find on video.

The more astute of you will notice that we have slipped in an extra genre. War films are in fact included largely within the Action/Adventure section of the guide itself.

■ ACTION/ADVENTURE
The Adventures of Robin Hood
Lawrence of Arabia
The Godfather
Jaws
Thelma and Louise
Romancing the Stone
Indiana Jones Trilogy
48 Hours
The Untouchables
The Fugitive

■ COMEDY
Bringing Up Baby
Gregory's Girl
To Be or Not To Be (1942)
Life Is Sweet
The Man with Two Brains
Tootsie
Ninotchka
A Fish Called Wanda
Monty Python's Life of Brian
Sleepless in Seattle

■ DRAMA
Citizen Kane
Gone With the Wind
Casablanca
The Third Man
Raging Bull
All About Eve
The Red Shoes
One Flew Over the Cuckoo's Nest
The Remains of the Day
Henry V (1989)

■ FAMILY
The Wizard of Oz
It's a Wonderful Life
The Railway Children
Great Expectations
Crocodile Dundee
Local Hero
Moonstruck
Field of Dreams
Home Alone
The Jungle Book

■ FOREIGN
La Regle du Jeu
Ran
The Seven Samurai
Cyrano de Bergerac
Women on the Verge of a Nervous
    Breakdown
Man Bites Dog
Jean de Florette/Manon des
    Sources
Farewell, My Concubine
Un Coeur en Hiver
Cinema Paradiso

■ HORROR
The Silence of the Lambs
An American Werewolf in London
Psycho
Misery
A Nightmare on Elm Street
The Omen
Cape Fear (1991)
The Hitcher
Halloween
Carrie

■ MUSICALS

Singin' in the Rain
High Society
Kiss Me Kate
Cabaret
The King and I
The Commitments
Seven Brides for Seven Brothers
Oklahoma!
The Sound of Music
Oliver!

■ MYSTERY/THRILLER

Witness
Jagged Edge
Reservoir Dogs
Suspect
Someone to Watch Over Me
Chinatown
The 39 Steps
In the Heat of the Night
The Maltese Falcon
Klute

■ SCI-FI/FANTASY

E.T. The Extra-Terrestrial
Close Encounters of the Third
    Kind
2001: A Space Odyssey
Star Wars Trilogy
Terminator 2
Back to the Future Trilogy
Alien/Aliens
Total Recall
Star Trek VI
Ghostbusters

■ WAR

Apocalypse Now
The Cruel Sea
M*A*S*H
The Bridge on the River Kwai
The Great Escape
Platoon
Zulu
The Dam Busters
A Bridge Too Far
All Quiet on the Western Front

■ WESTERNS

The Searchers
Stagecoach
Unforgiven
Butch Cassidy and the Sundance
    Kid
High Noon
Shane
The Magnificent Seven
Dances with Wolves
Red River
The Outlaw Josey Wales

USER GUIDE

Star rating	Title	Date first released		Running time	Certification

Leading actors

★★★ **Working Girl** 1988 113 mins (cert 15)

Sophisticated comedy of errors. *Melanie Griffith* is an upwardly-mobile secretary, *Sigourney Weaver* her ruthless boss. *Harrison Ford* provides the love interest.

Star ratings

★★★★★	Not to be missed
★★★★	Excellent
★★★	Very good
★★	Worth watching
★	OK

Certification

U	Universal
PG	Parental guidance
12	12 and over
15	15 and over
18	18 and over

ACTION/ADVENTURE

★★★ **Above Us the Waves** 1956   99 mins (cert U)
Gripping wartime drama of British submarine crew attempting
to destroy enemy ship. *John Mills* tops impressive cast.

★★★★★ **The Adventures of Robin Hood** 1938   102 mins (cert U)
Glorious swashbuckler with *Errol Flynn* as the dashing outlaw,
Olivia de Havilland a feisty Maid Marion and *Claude Raines* the
evil Prince John.

★★★★★ **The African Queen** 1951   103 mins (cert U)
Magnificent romantic adventure. Prissy missionary *Katharine
Hepburn* and drunken riverboat captain *Humphrey Bogart* brave a
treacherous journey down the Congo to destroy Nazi battleship.

★ **Air America** 1990   112 mins (cert 15)
Mel Gibson and *Robert Downey Jr* as CIA pilots in Vietnam. Weak
on the comedy; goodish action.

★★★ **Alive** 1993   121 mins (cert 15)
True story of plane crash survivors resorting to cannibalism to
stay alive during their long ordeal. Sensitive subject neatly
handled.

★★★★ **All Quiet on the Western Front** 1930   140 mins (cert PG)
Outstanding WWI drama examining the disillusionment of
young soldiers in the trenches.

★ **Another 48 Hours** 1990   95 mins (cert 18)
Eddie Murphy and *Nick Nolte*'s continuing love/hate relationship
as they take on the Iceman. Not a patch on the original.

★★★★ **Apocalypse Now** 1979   153 mins (cert 18)
Francis Coppola's hypnotic version of Joseph Conrad's 'Heart of
Darkness' set in Vietnam. Poignantly played by *Martin Sheen*,
Robert Duvall and *Marlon Brando*.

★★ **The Assassin** 1992   104 mins (cert 18)
Bridget Fonda as killer saved from execution by government
agent *Gabriel Byrne* in order to act as official hit woman. Able
support by *Harvey Keitel* and *Anne Bancroft*. Original French
version, 'Nikita', is better.

★★★ **Assault on Precinct 13** 1976   91 mins (cert 18)
John Carpenter's impressive modern-day 'Rio Bravo' set in LA
police station besieged by gang of youths. Tough, hard, violent.

★ **Backdraft** 1991   136 mins (cert 15)
Feuding firemen brothers, *Kurt Russell* and *William Baldwin*,
fight arsonist and each other. Mediocre story enlivened by
Robert De Niro as fire investigator; spectacular fire sequences.

★★★ **Ben Hur** 1959   217 mins (cert PG)
William Wyler's 11 Oscar epic pits *Charlton Heston*'s revenge-
seeking galley slave against the Romans. Somewhat earnest
story but marvellous chariot race.

★ **Best of the Best II** 1992   99 mins (cert 18)
Eric Roberts, *Christopher Penn* and *Philip Rhee* set up a martial arts
school and all goes nicely until Penn starts to dabble in the
underground world of kickboxing with tragic results.

★★★★ **Beverly Hills Cop** 1984   105 mins (cert 15)
Fast-talking, wise-cracking cop, *Eddie Murphy*, takes LA vacation
to find friend's killer. Highly enjoyable, undemanding and
humorous entertainment.

★★ **Beverly Hills Cop 2** 1987   99 mins (cert 15)
Dumb sequel that contains, if possible, even more movement
and violence but far less plot.

★★ **Blue Jean Cop** 1988   96 mins (cert 18)
Action movie in which a cop, *Peter Weller*, gets together with a
defence attorney to fight corruption in the police force.

★★★ **Blue Thunder** 1983   108 mins (cert 15)
Roy Scheider stars in an action movie that centres on the LA
police department's use of a super helicopter to take out the
bad guys.

★★★★ **Bonnie and Clyde** 1967   111 mins (cert 18)
Warren Beatty and *Faye Dunaway* as violent robbers on lawless
spree in the classic, mould-breaking 1960s movie.

★ **Bound and Gagged: A Love Story** 1993   100 mins (cert 18)
A road movie involving violence and lesbianism. Bound and
Gagged? I wish.

★★★★ **The Bounty** 1984   128 mins (cert 15)
Most convincing version of the story of the Bounty mutiny,
starring *Anthony Hopkins* and *Mel Gibson*.

....

★★★★ **The Bridge on the River Kwai** 1957   161 mins (cert U)
David Lean's powerful drama of POWs constructing bridge for
Japanese captors. *Alec Guinness* superb as the obsessed Colonel.

....

★★★★ **A Bridge Too Far** 1977   175 mins (cert 15)
Richard Attenborough's honest, star-studded portrayal of WWII
Allied operation to control the Rhine.

....

★★★ **Captain Blood** 1935   119 mins (cert U)
Errol Flynn as doctor turned dashing pirate. Plenty of romance,
sea battles and bags of swashing and buckling.

....

★ **Christopher Columbus: The Discovery** 1991   120 mins (cert PG)
George Corraface's Columbus heads out to sea as *Tom Selleck*'s
King of Spain gazes wistfully after him. *Marlon Brando* deserves
better than this. We all do.

....

★★★ **Cliffhanger** 1993   112 mins (cert 15)
Breathtaking stunts as ace mountaineer *Sylvester Stallone* chases
robber *John Lithgow* across treacherous mountain terrain. The
film that revived Stallone's career.

....

★★★ **The Colditz Story** 1954   97 mins (cert U)
British POWs plan to prove that 'escape proof' German castle is
anything but, in ever-popular wartime escape saga.

....

★★ **Convoy** 1978   115 mins (cert 15)
Daft but amiable Sam Peckinpah story of truckers striking
against oppression in trek across American south west.

....

★★ **The Corsican Brothers** 1942   112 mins (cert U)
Twins separated at birth remain emotionally attached in
entertaining version of Alexandre Dumas adventure.

....

★★★ **Cross of Iron** 1977   127 mins (cert 18)
Sam Peckinpah's WWII story of the officer determined to win
the Iron Cross. Excellent cast headed by *James Coburn* and
Maximilian Schell.

....

★★★★ **The Cruel Sea** 1953   126 mins (cert PG)
Gripping action/adventure involving the crew of a warship
during WWII. Among the best of British war films.

★★★ **The Dam Busters** 1954   125 mins (cert U)
Host of English actors grace exciting, intelligent WWII tale of
Barnes Wallace and his bouncing bomb. Brilliant music too.

★★ **Days of Thunder** 1990   107 mins (cert 12)
Tom Cruise and *Nicole Kidman* in a 'Top Gun' on the racing
circuit. Very flashy, but little substance. *Robert Duvall* lends
some much needed weight.

★★★ **D-Day the Sixth of June** 1956   106 mins (cert PG)
Lengthy romance set around the WWII Normandy invasion.
Robert Taylor leads the troops; *Dana Wynter* is the crumpet.

★★ **The Dead Pool** 1988   91 mins (cert 18)
Dirty Harry, *Clint Eastwood*, in his fifth, rather lacklustre,
outing; here investigating a bizarre death list.

★★★★ **Deliverance** 1972   109 mins (cert 18)
Horrifying events overtake *Burt Reynolds* and friends on canoe
trip through hillbilly country. This is easily Reynolds' best
performance – ever.

★★ **Demolition Man** 1993   114 mins (cert 15)
20th-century cop *Sylvester Stallone* and villain *Wesley Snipes* are
defrosted to pursue each other in 21st-century, crimeless society.
Some nice ideas never fully explored, though action's satisfying.

★★★ **The Desert Fox** 1951   88 mins (cert PG)
James Mason is superb as Field Marshal Rommel facing defeat,
disillusionment and death in desert warfare.

★★★ **The Desert Rats** 1953   88 mins (cert U)
Good star-studded tale of British captain, *Richard Burton*,
warding off German troops in North Africa. *James Mason* plays
Rommel again.

★★ **Diamonds Are Forever** 1971   120 mins (cert PG)
Sean Connery's penultimate outing as 007, this time in Las
Vegas. With *Jill St John* and *Charles Gray*. Otherwise the mixture
as before.

★★★★ **Die Hard** 1988   131 mins (cert 18)
Excellent action/drama stars *Bruce Willis* as wise-cracking cop
single-handedly battling terrorists. *Alan Rickman* makes a great
heavy.

★★ **Die Hard 2** 1990   120 mins (cert 15)
Bruce Willis returns to take on terrorists, this time at Dulles airport. Same as before, though not as much fun. Willis does seem to be in the wrong place at the wrong time more often than is good for him.

★★★ **The Dirty Dozen** 1967   150 mins (cert 15)
Macho, stellar cast play hard-case jailbirds sent to infiltrate enemy lines to redeem themselves in wartime action/adventure.

★★★★ **Dirty Harry** 1971   103 mins (cert 18)
First and best outing for *Clint Eastwood* as the magnum-packing, sharp-shooting detective assigned to bring in crazed killer.

★★ **Double Impact** 1991   100 mins (cert 18)
Twins – *Jean-Claude Van Damme* twice – separated at birth reunite to avenge their parents' murder by the Triads. Corny plot and dialogue. Good action, though.

★★ **Downhill Racer** 1969   102mins (cert PG)
Robert Redford in an anti-hero role as the ambitious but disagreeable skier looking for a place in the US Olympic team.

★★★ **Dragon: The Bruce Lee Story** 1993   121 mins (cert 15)
Excellent depiction of kung fu karate king by *Jason Scott Lee* (no relation) in gripping story combining action and romance.

★★ **The Driver** 1978   90 mins (cert 15)
Car chases are the best thing in action/drama with *Ryan O'Neal* as professional getaway driver up against cop, *Bruce Dern*.

★★★ **Dr No** 1962   111 mins (cert PG)
First of the Bond movies sees *Sean Connery* creating 007. Still one of the series' best.

★★ **The Eagle Has Landed** 1977   135 mins (cert 15)
Nazi plot to assassinate Churchill provides reasonable star vehicle for likes of *Michael Caine*, *Robert Duvall* and *Donald Sutherland*.

★★ **El Cid** 1961   184 mins (cert U)
Spectacular action movie sees the Spanish hero, *Charlton Heston*, romancing *Sophia Loren* as he attempts to drive the Moors from his country.

★★ The Enforcer 1976   96 mins (cert 18)
Dirty Harry Callahan, *Clint Eastwood*, and female partner *Tyne Daly* on the trail of terrorists. Third in the Dirty Harry series and looking tired.

....

★★★ Escape from Alcatraz 1979   112 mins (cert 15)
Reasonable action yarn with *Clint Eastwood* escaping from the reputedly ultra-secure prison in story based on fact.

....

★★ Escape from Sobibor 1987   142 mins (cert 15)
Alan Arkin leads biggest escape ever attempted from a Nazi concentration camp in solid, made-for-TV movie.

....

★★★ Excalibur 1981   140 mins (cert 15)
John Boorman's lavish, quirky rendition of King Arthur fable. The cast is both impressive and surprising.

....

★ The Exterminator 1980   101 mins (cert 18)
Violent vigilante, *Robert Ginty*, wreaking revenge on gang that paralysed friend. Run-of-the-mill mayhem.

....

★★ Firefox 1982   127 mins (cert 12)
Unconvincing *Clint Eastwood* Cold War vehicle in which Clint plays US pilot sent to Moscow to steal state-of-the-art Russian jet fighter.

....

★★★ The First of the Few 1942   117 mins (cert U)
Impressive biopic starring *Leslie Howard* and depicting life of R J Mitchell and events surrounding his invention of the Spitfire.

....

★★★★ 48 Hours 1982   97 mins (cert 18)
Sharp, fast thriller in which cop *Nick Nolte* 'borrows' jailed conman *Eddie Murphy* for two days to help catch a cop killer.

....

★★ For Your Eyes Only 1981   127 mins (cert PG)
Roger Moore as 007. Stunts and traditional action replace earlier technical wizardry.

....

★★★★ From Here to Eternity 1953   118 mins (cert PG)
Pre-WWII American military drama. Excellent performances by *Burt Lancaster*, *Deborah Kerr* and *Frank Sinatra*. Best remembered for sizzling sex scene on beach.

★★★ **From Russia With Love** 1963   118 mins (cert PG)
Sean Connery as James Bond nicely supported by *Robert Shaw* as psycho assassin.

★★★★ **The Fugitive** 1993   140 mins (cert 12)
Brilliant action/adventure based on TV series. *Harrison Ford* as the innocent doctor on the run for murdering his wife and ardently pursued by sheriff, *Tommy Lee Jones*. Fantastic, fun and exciting.

★★★ **Full Metal Jacket** 1987   116 mins (cert 18)
Stanley Kubrick's contribution to Vietnam war movies shows *Matthew Modine* undergoing the horrors of training and actual warfare.

★★ **Funeral in Berlin** 1966   102 mins (cert PG)
Sequel to 'The Ipcress File'. *Michael Caine* reprises role of Harry Palmer in sharp spy drama.

★★★ **FX: Murder by Illusion** 1986   107 mins (cert 15)
Fast-paced caper about movie special effects man hired to protect a supergrass. *Bryan Brown* and *Brian Dennehy* star.

★★ **FX 2: The Deadly Art of Illusion** 1991   109 mins (cert 15)
Mixture much as before – *Bryan Brown* again using his skills to give the cops (especially *Brian Dennehy*) a hand. Just as well he never seems to have a movie to make.

★★★ **Gallipoli** 1981   110 mins (cert PG)
Gripping study of the people and events involved in futile, suicidal WWI Australian campaign against Turks. *Mel Gibson* at his best under Peter Weir's direction.

★★★ **The Gauntlet** 1977   109 mins (cert 18)
Fast-paced and fairly preposterous action movie directed by and starring *Clint Eastwood* as cop escorting prostitute, *Sondra Locke*, to testify at trial.

★★★ **Glory** 1989   122 mins (cert 15)
Harrowing account of first black regiment in American Civil War. *Matthew Broderick* and *Denzel Washington* excellent, as are battle scenes.

★★★★★ **The Godfather** 1972   175 mins (cert 18)
Best gangster movie ever made. Definitive Mafia story awash
with talent. Francis Coppola directs. *Marlon Brando*, *Al Pacino*
and *James Caan* head Corleone family.

....

★★★★★ **The Godfather Part II** 1974   200 mins (cert 18)
Only sequel to match its forerunner continues Corleone saga
minus James Caan. Compelling story of corruption of power.

....

★★★ **The Godfather Part III** 1990   160 mins (cert 15)
Most lavish but weakest of the family series. Still worth
watching if only for *Andy Garcia*.

....

★★ **Goldfinger** 1964   112 mins (cert PG)
Sean Connery, licensed to kill, takes on evil *Gert Frobe*. *Honor
Blackman* is the unusually feisty Bond girl.

....

★★★★ **Goodfellas** 1990   146 mins (cert 18)
Martin Scorsese's violent, riveting depiction of Mafia soldiers in
New York. Explosive performance from *Joe Pesci*; *Robert De Niro*
and *Ray Liotta* give excellent support.

....

★★★★★ **The Great Escape** 1963   173 mins (cert PG)
Plethora of stars play Allied POWs masterminding mass
breakout from WWII German concentration camp.

....

★★ **Greystoke: The Legend of Tarzan** 1984   129 mins (cert PG)
Rich and faithful version of the Tarzan story. *Christopher
Lambert*'s the man raised by apes, *Ralph Richardson* his baronial
uncle bringing him home.

....

★★★ **Gunga Din** 1939   117 mins (cert U)
Ripping yarn with *Cary Grant*, *Douglas Fairbanks Jr* and *Victor
McLaglen* as three soldier comrades involved in 19th-century
uprising in India. Owes little to Rudyard Kipling.

....

★★★ **The Guns of Navarone** 1961   157 mins (cert U)
Multi-national commandos are dispatched to destroy WWII
German gun. Cracking action/adventure with *Gregory Peck*,
David Niven and *Richard Harris*.

★ **Hard Target** 1993   95 mins (cert 18)
Ridiculous shoot-'em-up in which *Jean-Claude Van Damme*
uncovers a fatal man-hunt racket. Despite facing an army of
baddies and an arsenal that would put the US army's to shame,
our hero emerges without so much as a graze – we're talking
macho!

★★ **Heartbreak Ridge** 1986   130 mins (cert 15)
Muscular army action stuff from *Clint Eastwood* as grizzled
sergeant knocking rookies into shape before they invade
Grenada, for God's sake. I mean, that was hardly the world's
most important war.

★★★ **High Sierra** 1941   96 mins (cert PG)
Somewhat overplotted action/film noir with strong lead
performances from *Humphrey Bogart* and *Ida Lupino*.

★★★ **The Hunt for Red October** 1990   135 mins (cert PG)
Exciting suspense thriller about a Soviet naval captain, *Sean
Connery*, stealing a state-of-the-art nuclear submarine to help
him defect to the west.

★★★ **Ice Cold in Alex** 1960   129 mins (cert PG)
John Mills stranded in desert in charge of ambulance, a nurse
and a Nazi soldier. Splendid WWII action adventure.

★★★★ **Indiana Jones and the Last Crusade** 1989   127 mins (cert PG)
Best of the series sees *Harrison Ford* searching for his father,
Sean Connery, and the Holy Grail.

★★ **Indiana Jones and the Temple of Doom** 1984   117 mins (cert PG)
Weakish sequel to 'Raiders of the Lost Ark'. *Harrison Ford* as
Jones, *Kate Capshaw* as Jones's girl.

★★ **An Innocent Man** 1989   114 mins (cert 18)
Brutal, overlong action movie. *Tom Selleck* wrongly imprisoned
and out for justice and revenge.

★★★ **In the Line of Fire** 1993   118 mins (cert 15)
Clint Eastwood as the veteran FBI agent charged with protecting
the US president against murderous sociopath *John Malkovich*.
Good stunts, good performances.

★★★ **Into the West** 1992   102 mins (cert PG)
Two young Irish boys save a horse and flee to the coast followed
by father *Gabriel Byrne*, gypsy *Ellen Barkin* and police. Magical,
mystical and pleasing.

★★★ **In Which We Serve** 1942   114 mins (cert U)
Noel Coward's WWII drama centring on the survivors of a
torpedoed destroyer. Dated but still splendid. *Richard
Attenborough* makes his debut.

★★★ **The Italian Job** 1969   100 mins (cert U)
Michael Caine and *Noel Coward* in crime caper. Complicated plot
involves creating world's biggest traffic jam in Rome. Good fun.

★★ **I Was Monty's Double** 1958   100 mins (cert U)
True WWII story of actor, *Clifton James*, recruited to
impersonate Field Marshal Montgomery in a bid to fool the
Nazis.

★★★★★ **Jaws** 1975   125 mins (cert PG)
Spielberg's terrific thriller of seaside resort terrorised by shark.
Roy Scheider, *Robert Shaw* and *Richard Dreyfuss* as both hunters
and hunted. If you haven't seen it, you haven't lived – and you
certainly shouldn't go swimming.

★★ **Jaws 2** 1978   117 mins (cert PG)
Scheider's back again, so's the shark, in just about adequate
reprise of the original. (Two further sequels – 'Jaws 3D' with
Dennis Quaid and 3D effects and 'Jaws 4' with *Michael Caine* – are
unworthy of attention.)

★★★ **Jeremiah Johnson** 1972   107 mins (cert PG)
Rambling, often gripping tale of mountain man, *Robert Redford*,
surviving the wilderness in 1850s Utah. One of Redford's best
performances.

★★★ **The Jewel of the Nile** 1985   104 mins (cert PG)
Fast-paced but slight sequel to 'Romancing the Stone'. *Kathleen
Turner*, *Michael Douglas* and *Danny DeVito* reprise roles.

★★★ **The Karate Kid** 1984   126 mins (cert PG)
Bullied teenager, *Ralph Macchio*, turns on tormentors when
Japanese handyman, *Pat Morita*, teaches him the martial arts.
(Two sequels provide more of the same, less entertainingly.)

★★ **Kickboxer** 1989   100 mins (cert 18)
Violent karate champ, *Jean-Claude Van Damme*, swears revenge
on the kickboxer who maimed his brother. Fairly vicious stuff
notable, if at all, as Van Damme's first starring vehicle.

★★ **Kid** 1990   91 mins (cert 18)
Sort of contemporary update of 'High Plains Drifter'. *C Thomas
Howell* alights from a bus in a small western town to avenge his
dead parents. Pretty violent but some humour.

★★★ **Kindergarten Cop** 1990   111 mins (cert 12)
Mean policeman, *Arnold Schwarzenegger*, goes undercover as
primary school teacher in a tale too violent to be funny.

★★ **King Kong** 1976   135 mins (cert PG)
Good special effects and sympathetic attitude towards gorilla in
competent remake. *Jessica Lange*, on her debut, reprises Fay
Wray's role.

★★ **King of New York** 1990   103 mins (cert 18)
An excessively violent film but a powerful performance by
Christopher Walken as a newly-released prisoner taking on New
York's druglords.

★★ **K9** 1989   102 mins (cert 15)
Alsatian and cop, *James Belushi*, pal up to catch drug pushers in
feeble action movie.

★★★ **The Krays** 1990   119 mins (cert 18)
Hard-hitting portrait of the psychotic Cockney brothers who
ruled London's East End underworld. The Spandau Ballet
brothers, *Gary Kemp* and *Martin Kemp*, surprisingly good as
Reggie and Ron.

★★ **Kuffs** 1991   102 mins (cert 15)
Christian Slater takes over his dead brother's San Francisco
private police force in a decidedly soppy teenage action flick.
Slater fans will probably like it, though.

★★ **Last Action Hero** 1993   136 mins (cert 15)
A magic cinema ticket enables young lad to enter cinema screen
but also lets movie hero *Arnold Schwarzenegger* and evil *Charles
Dance* come out. Despite numerous star cameos, film spoofs and
money oozing from every stunt pore, it's downright dull.

★★★ **The Last Boy Scout** 1991   105 mins (cert 18)
Ultra-violent action/thriller pickled with comic one-liners and hectic car chases. *Bruce Willis* stars as down-at-heel PI; *Daman Wayans* is his ex-footballer sidekick.

★★★★ **The Last of the Mohicans** 1992   122 mins (cert 12)
Superb adventure. *Daniel Day-Lewis* helping English colonel's daughters, *Madeleine Stowe* and *Jodhi May*, through war-torn and Indian-infested American frontier in 1757. *Wes Studi* gives us one of modern cinema's nastiest villains.

★★★★ **Lawrence of Arabia** 1962   222 mins (cert PG)
David Lean's magnificent epic which brought instant stardom to *Peter O'Toole* as the enigmatic adventurer.

★★★ **Lethal Weapon** 1987   110 mins (cert 18)
Fast-action cops and robbers pairing *Mel Gibson* and *Danny Glover* as the good guys. Violent, trashy and fun.

★★ **Lethal Weapon 2** 1989   111 mins (cert 15)
Inevitable sequel to the above. Perhaps even more violent. Again *Gibson* and *Glover* risk all to catch baddies.

★★★★ **Lethal Weapon 3** 1992   118 mins (cert 15)
Best of the series. More humour accompanies the action as a story of police corruption unravels. *Joe Pesci* returns as *Gibson* and *Glover*'s hapless side-kick.

★ **Licence to Kill** 1989   133 mins (cert 15)
Timothy Dalton as 007 again; *Robert Davi* particularly good as the heavy; *Carey Lowell* the more than usually liberated crumpet. Otherwise the mixture as before.

★★★ **Little Caesar** 1930   80 mins (cert PG)
Edward G Robinson shot to stardom in this dated but classic 1930s gangster movie based loosely on the exploits of Al Capone. His 'Is this the end of Rico?' is one of the great lines of the movies.

★★ **Live and Let Die** 1973   121 mins (cert PG)
First licence to kill for *Roger Moore* as James Bond. Lots of wild chase sequences. Paul McCartney title song.

★★ **Lock-Up** 1989   106 mins (cert 18)
Violent, soppy thriller with convict, *Sylvester Stallone*, persecuted by jail governor, *Donald Sutherland*.

★★★ **The Long and the Short and the Tall** 1961   105 mins (cert 18)
Vivid war drama of British patrol in Malayan jungle. *Laurence Harvey* rather miscast but *Richard Todd* and *Richard Harris* first rate.

★★★ **The Longest Day** 1962   169 mins (cert PG)
Mammoth re-creation of Allied invasion of Normandy. Stirring battle scenes and all-star cast: *John Wayne*, *Henry Fonda*, *Robert Mitchum*, *Sean Connery*, *Richard Burton*, etc.

★★★★ **The Long Good Friday** 1980   105 mins (cert 18)
Tough, exciting British gangster thriller. Great performance by *Bob Hoskins*; fine support from *Helen Mirren*.

★★ **Mad Max** 1979   105 mins (cert 18)
Futuristic, innovative action movie. *Mel Gibson* is the policeman out to avenge the murder of wife and child.

★★ **Mad Max 2: The Road Warrior** 1981   90 mins (cert 18)
Visually impressive, action-filled sequel sees *Gibson* protecting small community against marauding group.

★★★ **Mad Max 3: Beyond Thunderdome** 1985   107 mins (cert 15)
Gibson's futuristic warrior exiled to desert. Stunts, chases and *Tina Turner* flesh it out a bit.

★★★ **Magnum Force** 1973   124 mins (cert 18)
Clint Eastwood's second outing as Dirty Harry. Not quite up to the original but still gripping as Clint hunts down murderous cops.

★★★ **The Man Who Would Be King** 1975   129 mins (cert PG)
Splendid John Huston version of Kipling story. *Sean Connery* and *Michael Caine* as British soldiers conning Indian priests of riches.

★★★ **Married to the Mob** 1988   104 mins (cert 15)
Enjoyable comic adventure of gangster's moll, *Michelle Pfeiffer*, trying to cut ties from the Mob. *Matthew Modine* is her police protector.

★★★ **McVicar** 1980   112 mins (cert 18)
Roger Daltrey is rather good as convicted, then escaped, then rehabilitated murderer. Based on McVicar's own book.

★★★★ **Mean Streets** 1973   110 mins (cert 18)
Martin Scorsese's riveting study of young hoods in Little Italy. With *Robert De Niro* and *Harvey Keitel*.

★★★ **Memphis Belle** 1990   107 mins (cert 12)
Spectacular dramatisation of the 25th and final mission of B52 bomber crew during WWII. Young male talent form crew.

★ **Mobsters: The Evil Empire** 1991   121 mins (cert 18)
Christian Slater leads dim, Brat Pack gangster movie about the rise of Lucky Luciano. 'The Godfather' it ain't.

★★★ **Moonraker** 1979   126 mins (cert PG)
Roger Moore as 007 in James Bond adventure that increasingly resembles an animated comic strip with gadgets. *Michael Lonsdale* makes a good, weighty heavy.

★★★★ **Mutiny on the Bounty** 1935   135 mins (cert U)
Charles Laughton at his most splendidly hateful as Captain Bligh; *Clark Gable* charismatic as mutiny leader, Fletcher Christian.

★★ **Mutiny on the Bounty** 1962   177 mins (cert 15)
Disappointing remake, this time with *Trevor Howard* as Bligh and *Marlon Brando* as Fletcher Christian.

★★★ **The Name of the Rose** 1986   131 mins (cert 18)
Atmospheric mystery story of a monk turned detective. *Sean Connery* investigates murders in a 14th-century monastery. Early appearance by a young *Christian Slater*.

★★ **Navy Seals** 1990   113 mins (cert 15)
Dreary action/thriller with *Charlie Sheen* and *Michael Biehn* as members of the US Marines' crack commando unit.

★★★ **Never Say Never Again** 1983   134 mins (cert PG)
Sean Connery returns as Bond, certainly for the last time, in a stylish but overlong remake of 'Thunderball'.

★ **New Jack City** 1991   100 mins (cert 18)
Poor thriller with *Wesley Snipes* as New York drug baron. Predictability and stereotypes wherever you look.

★★ **Next of Kin** 1989   108 mins (cert 15)
Patrick Swayze as a country cop tracking down mean mobster
Adam Baldwin through the rougher parts of Chicago. *Liam Neeson*
as Swayze's brother.

★★ **Nico: Above the Law** 1988   99 mins (cert 18)
Steven Seagal flexes the occasional muscle in undemanding role
as Chicago cop out to protect a senator. Not much demanded of
the viewer's brain either.

★★★★ **North by Northwest** 1959   136 mins (cert PG)
Sparkling Hitchcock adventure with *Cary Grant* as innocuous
advertising executive mistaken for spy.

★★★★ **Northwest Frontier** 1959   129 mins (cert U)
Kenneth More as dashing British soldier guiding train bearing
native prince through war-torn India. *Lauren Bacall*, *Herbert Lom*
and *Wilfrid Hyde White* are among the other passengers. Great
Empire stuff. Lips never stiffer.

★ **Nowhere to Run** 1992   95 mins (cert 15)
Nowhere to hide. Outlaw *Jean-Claude Van Damme* helps *Rosanna
Arquette* defend her homestead against evil property developer,
Joss Ackland.

★★★ **Octopussy** 1983   130 mins (cert PG)
Thirteenth James Bond movie sees *Roger Moore* smoothly
outwitting the evil *Maud Adams* and dastardly plot to nuke US
forces.

★★ **The Package** 1989   108 mins (cert 15)
Gene Hackman becomes the fall guy in an East/West Cold War
conspiracy while conducting prisoner *Tommy Lee Jones* to
Washington.

★★★ **Papillon** 1973   150 mins (cert 18)
Outstanding performances by *Dustin Hoffman* and *Steve McQueen*
in overlong story of prisoner's escape from Devil's Island.

★★ **Passenger 57** 1993   84 mins (cert 15)
Wesley Snipes as an airline cop on board a plane hijacked by
psychotic *Bruce Payne* on way to trial. Rather appealing, though
corny and predictable.

★★ **Patriot Games** 1992   117 mins (cert 15)
Harrison Ford foils IRA plot to blow up MP *James Fox*, so he and
wife, *Anne Archer*, become targets of terrorist *Sean Bean*. Daft but
quite exciting.

★★★ **Patton: Lust for Glory** 1970   173 mins (cert PG)
George C Scott superb in biopic of feisty, eccentric US general in
WWII.

★★★★ **A Perfect World** 1993   135 mins (cert 12)
Kevin Costner as an escaped convict forming a relationship with
the young boy he takes hostage. *Clint Eastwood* doubles as the
Texas Ranger on his trail and director.

★★★ **Platoon** 1986   120 mins (cert 15)
Oliver Stone's harrowing depiction of US soldiers' lives – and
their atrocities – during Vietnam war.

★ **Point Break** 1991   120 mins (cert 15)
Ludicrous action picture about surfing bank robbers. With
Patrick Swayze and *Keanu Reeves* riding those tubes.

★★★ **The Poseidon Adventure** 1972   117 mins (cert PG)
Disaster movie on the high seas as starry cast panic aboard
sinking liner. Oscar-winning special effects.

★★ **Predator** 1987   107 mins (cert 18)
Arnold Schwarzenegger heads SWAT team on rescue mission in
jungle, but someone or something keeps killing them.

★★ **Predator 2** 1990   108 mins (cert 18)
Frenetic sequel, this time with *Danny Glover* and *Gary Busey* up
against the predator on the streets of LA.

★★ **The Prisoner of Zenda** 1952   100 mins (cert U)
Very acceptable re-make of classic 1937 Ronald Colman movie.
This time starring *Stewart Granger*.

★★ **Quigley Down Under** 1990   120 mins (cert 12)
Tom Selleck arrives in turn-of-century Australia as trouble
shooter for evil ranch owner *Alan Rickman* – easily the best thing
in it. A Western Down Under.

★★ **A Rage in Harlem** 1991　　　110 mins (cert 18)
Racy, sometimes effective combination of sex and violence in
quest for stolen gold in 1950s Harlem.

★★★★ **Raiders of the Lost Ark** 1981　　　115 mins (cert PG)
First rousing adventure of intrepid archaeologist Indiana Jones,
Harrison Ford. Expertly directed by Steven Spielberg.

★★ **Rapid Fire** 1992　　　95 mins (cert 18)
The late *Brandon Lee* – son of Bruce – brings class to typical
kung fu action/thriller.

★★★ **Reach for the Sky** 1956　　　135 mins (cert U)
Solid account of exploits of WWII flying ace, Douglas Bader –
Kenneth Moore – who heroically overcame the handicap of a
double leg amputation.

★★★ **The Red Badge of Courage** 1951　　　69 mins (cert U)
John Huston's American Civil War story – truncated and nearly
massacred by MGM – with *Audie Murphy* as the young soldier
guilt-stricken over his cowardice.

★★ **Red Heat** 1991　　　104 mins (cert 18)
Arnold Schwarzenegger as Russian cop sent to Chicago to partner
James Belushi on hunt for Red drug pusher. Not as much violence
as you'd expect from director Walter Hill but authentic – first
film shot in Red Square.

★ **Revenge** 1990　　　124 mins (cert 18)
Set in wilds of Mexico where *Kevin Costner* goes to stay with
wealthy rancher *Anthony Quinn* but falls for his abused wife,
Madeleine Stowe. Soon turns from romantic thriller to brutal,
boring chase.

★★★ **The Right Stuff** 1983　　　193 mins (cert 15)
Story of first American astronauts in a sort of space Western
adapted from Tom Wolfe's bestseller. Better than its box-office
performance would suggest.

★★ **Road House** 1989　　　114 mins (cert 18)
Patrick Swayze as a nightclub bouncer with a remarkable (and
unlikely) past charged with cleaning up a Missouri road house.
Lots of violent action.

★★★ **The Roaring Twenties** 1939   106 mins (cert PG)
Dated but still classic gangster story. *James Cagney* and *Humphrey Bogart* involved with the rackets after WWI.

★★ **Robin Hood** 1991   104 mins (cert PG)
Not the most exciting bunch of merry men led by a downright dull Robin. *Patrick Bergin*, devoid of sex appeal, doesn't deserve *Uma Thurman*'s Maid Marian.

★★★ **Robin Hood: Prince of Thieves** 1991   143 mins (cert PG)
Kevin Costner's earnest folk hero is totally overshadowed by *Alan Rickman*'s gloriously hammy Sheriff of Nottingham.

★★ **Robocop** 1987   103 mins (cert 18)
Peter Weller as half-man, half-cyborg law-keeper. Distastefully violent but may just be worth watching for the special effects.

★★ **Robocop II** 1990   102 mins (cert 18)
Rather less violent than its predecessor as the Robocop comes up against an even more destructive mechanical monster.

★★ **The Rocketeer** 1991   120 mins (cert PG)
Amiable, 1930s spoof in which a unique flying machine brings adventures and danger for pilot hero. *Bill Campbell* and *Jennifer Connolly* star.

★★★ **Rocky** 1976   119 mins (cert PG)
Raw energy emanates from *Sylvester Stallone*'s portrayal of small-time fighter given a shot at the title. Best of the series.

★★ **Rocky 2** 1979   119 mins (cert PG)
Adequate sequel continues much along lines of original. But by now we've seen it all before.

★★ **Rocky 3** 1982   99 mins (cert PG)
And we see it all again as Rocky loses title to Mr T and goes for the re-match.

★ **Rocky 4** 1985   91 mins (cert PG)
Utter nonsense as Rocky avenges his friend's death and fights for world peace against Russian champ *Dolph Lundgren*.

★ **Rocky 5** 1990   104 mins (cert PG)
Not that you'd notice, but the champ has suffered brain damage; worse, he's lost all his money. But by now nobody cares.

★★★ **Romancing the Stone** 1984   105 mins (cert PG)
Romantic adventure. Novelist *Kathleen Turner* involved with
Michael Douglas in search for kidnapped sister in South America.
Fast, enjoyable and a lot of fun.

★ **Romper Stomper** 1992   91 mins (cert 18)
Vicious drama about Australian skinheads and racism.
Alienating but energetic and sometimes thought-provoking.

★★ **Rumble Fish** 1983   94 mins (cert 18)
Intense, over-stylised drama of alienated teenager, *Matt Dillon*,
manipulated by older brother, *Mickey Rourke*.

★★★ **The Sea Hawk** 1940   122 mins (cert U)
Errol Flynn cuts a dashing blade as Sir Francis Drake. *Flora
Robson* plays Elizabeth I. Good, swashbuckling stuff.

★ **Shanghai Surprise** 1986   97 mins (cert 15)
Pretty dire romantic adventure featuring *Madonna* and her then
husband *Sean Penn*. Feeble plot, feeble performances.

★★ **Shining Through** 1992   132 mins (cert 15)
So bad it's funny. *Melanie Griffith* as a spy in Germany during
WWII. *Michael Douglas* is the woefully negligent intelligence
officer who sent her there. Hilariously absurd.

★★★ **Slap Shot** 1977   124 mins (cert 18)
Quick-fire comedy of minor league ice hockey team which,
under player-coach *Paul Newman*, learns to play – and talk –
dirty and start winning.

★★★ **Sneakers** 1992   125 mins (cert 12)
Great caper movie with starry cast, wonderful gadgetry and
clever plot. *Robert Redford* and *River Phoenix* lead the good guys;
Ben Kingsley is the baddy out to rule the world.

★★ **Sniper** 1992   98 mins (cert 15)
US army snipers *Tom Berenger* and *Billy Zane*, on a killing
mission in hostile jungle, bicker their way tediously through the
bush.

★★★ **The Sound Barrier** 1952   118 mins (cert U)
Soaring cinematography, solid performances by *Ralph Richardson*
and *Ann Todd*, plus David Lean's direction distinguish this tale
of the men who tested the early jet planes.

★★★ **South Central** 1992   99 mins (cert 15)
Black gang culture explored in a sincere and thoughtful study of the dangers of life in the ghetto.

★★★★ **Southern Comfort** 1981   106 mins (cert 18)
Intense, survival-of-the-fittest yarn based on National Guardsmen caught in guerrilla warfare in the Louisiana swamps. Terrific atmosphere and taut direction by Walter Hill.

★★★ **Spartacus** 1960   196 mins (cert PG)
Spectacular story of the slave, *Kirk Douglas*, who led a rebellion against Rome. Good support from the likes of *Laurence Olivier*, *Tony Curtis* and *Peter Ustinov*.

★ **Spymaker: The Secret Life of Ian Fleming** 1990   100 mins (cert 15)
Weak, fictionalised biography of the creator of James Bond. Nice touch, though, to cast Sean Connery's son, *Jason Connery*, in the title role.

★★★ **The Spy Who Loved Me** 1977   125 mins (cert PG)
One of the best Bond movies pits *Roger Moore* and *Barbara Bach* against indestructible adversary, Jaws – *Richard Kiel*.

★★★★ **Stalag 17** 1953   120 mins (cert PG)
Brilliant blend of drama, excitement and wit in Billy Wilder's tale of Americans in a German POW camp. Probably *William Holden*'s best performance.

★★★ **Streets of Fire** 1984   94 mins (cert 15)
Prettier to look at than listen to. Rock 'n' roll fantasy with *Michael Pare* fighting to free girlfriend *Diane Lane* from kidnappers.

★★ **Super Mario Brothers** 1992   105 mins (cert PG)
You've played the video game – now see the movie. Not that it's up to much, alas. *Bob Hoskins* and *John Leguizamo* are the two Brooklyn plumbers plunged into a parallel world to save *Samantha Mathis*.

★★★ **The Taking of Pelham 123** 1974   104 mins (cert 15)
Robert Shaw hijacks a New York subway train, holding the passengers to ransom. *Walter Matthau* has a tension-packed hour to free them.

★★★★ **A Tale of Two Cities** 1935   121 mins (cert U)
Lavish version of Charles Dickens' classic story of the French Revolution. *Ronald Colman* and *Elizabeth Allan* lead.

★★ **Tango and Cash** 1989   104 mins (cert 15)
Mediocre action movie about two policemen, *Kurt Russell* and *Sylvester Stallone*, at loggerheads over different attitudes to profession.

········

★★ **Teenage Mutant Ninja Turtles** 1990   93 mins (cert PG)
Four mutated turtles – Leonardo, Donatello, Raphael and Michelangelo – fight New York crimewave from their home in the sewers. So-so mix of action and comedy.

········

★★ **Teenage Mutant Ninja Turtles II** 1991   87 mins (cert PG)
Pizza-loving dudes return to wage war on toxic waste. Young viewers should find it as pleasing – or not – as the first.

········

★★ **Teenage Mutant Ninja Turtles III** 1992   95 mins (cert PG)
Mixture as before as the overgrown terrapins go back in time to ancient Japan to rescue April, *Paige Turco*.

········

★★★★ **The Ten Commandments** 1956   219 mins (cert U)
Cecil B DeMille's biblical epic. Cast of thousands. *Charlton Heston* as Moses, *Yul Brynner* as Pharaoh.

········

★★★★★ **Thelma and Louise** 1991   130 mins (cert 15)
A smashing movie. Great photography, superb direction by Ridley Scott and outstanding performances by *Geena Davis* and *Susan Sarandon* as two rebellious women having a ball on the run for murder.

········

★★★★ **The Three Musketeers** 1973   107 mins (cert U)
Entertaining, tongue-in-cheek version of the romantic swashbuckler with *Oliver Reed*, *Richard Chamberlain*, *Michael York*, *Raquel Welch*, *Charlton Heston* and *Faye Dunaway*.

········

★ **The Three Musketeers** 1993   106 mins (cert PG)
Kiefer Sutherland, *Charlie Sheen* and *Chris O'Donnell* buckle badly rather than swash in this unnecessary and inept remake.

········

★★★ **Three Ninja Kids** 1992   85 mins (cert PG)
Three kids are taught the martial arts by Oriental grandad and use them to help their FBI agent father foil evil arms importers.

········

★★★ **Thunderball** 1965   132 mins (cert PG)
The fourth in the Bond series and still good value. *Sean Connery* as 007, *Adolfi Celli* the evil Largo. Connery did it all again in the remake, 'Never Say Never Again'.

★★★★ **To Have and Have Not** 1944   100 mins (cert 15)
A sort of Howard Hawkes version of 'Casablanca'. *Humphrey Bogart* reluctantly embroiled with French Resistance while wooing *Lauren Bacall*.

....

★★★ **Top Gun** 1986   110 mins (cert 15)
Young naval pilot, *Tom Cruise*, conducts passionate love affair with *Kelly McGillis* against backdrop of incredible flying sequences.

....

★★★ **Tora! Tora! Tora!** 1970   144 mins (cert U)
Tense action movie portraying events leading to attack on Pearl Harbour from both American and Japanese points of view.

....

★★★ **The Towering Inferno** 1974   165 mins (cert 15)
Contrived disaster movie, enhanced by good effects and an expensive cast: *Paul Newman*, *Steve McQueen*, *Fred Astaire*, *Faye Dunaway*, et al.

....

★★★ **A Town Like Alice** 1956   117 mins (cert U)
Powerful story of female POWs in Malaysia, headed by *Virginia McKenna* and helped by the man from Alice Springs, *Peter Finch*. Nicely romantic.

....

★★★ **Toy Soldiers** 1991   112 mins (cert 15)
Problem preppies – *Sean Astin*, et al – show astonishing ingenuity when their school is hijacked by terrorists. Enjoyable, though much suspension of disbelief required.

....

★★★ **Trespass** 1992   101 mins (cert 18)
Two white firemen, *Bill Paxton* and *William Sadler*, hunting for treasure in a disused warehouse run into a drugs gang – *Ice T* and *Ice Cube* among them – with violent results.

....

★★★★ **True Romance** 1993   119 mins (cert 18)
Brilliant, violent black comedy by Quentin Tarantino. *Christian Slater* and *Patricia Arquette* head for LA with cache of cocaine and the Mafia in pursuit. Splendid cameo performances by *Gary Oldman*, *Dennis Hopper* and *Christopher Walken*.

....

★★★★ **Twelve O'Clock High** 1949   132 mins (cert U)
Great performances by *Gregory Peck* and *Dean Jagger* in taut absorbing story of American bomber crews based in England during WWII.

★★ **Under Siege** 1992   103 mins (cert 15)
Sea cook *Steven Seagal* single-handedly rescues his battleship
from potential world-destroyer, *Tommy Lee Jones*. Action from
Seagal, acting class from Jones.

....

★★★★ **The Untouchables** 1987   119 mins (cert 15)
Prohibition Chicago's the setting for FBI agent Elliot Ness,
Kevin Costner, to bring down Al Capone, *Robert De Niro*, with the
help of policeman, *Sean Connery*. Taut Brian De Palma thriller.

....

★★★ **A View to a Kill** 1985   121 mins (cert PG)
Roger Moore as Bond, *Christopher Walken* as the villain seeking to
corner the world's microchip supply.

....

★★★★ **Viva Zapata!** 1952   112 mins (cert PG)
Marlon Brando gives outstanding portrayal of the legendary
Mexican revolutionary who rose to the presidency.

....

★★★ **War and Peace** 1956   208 mins (cert U)
Simplified King Vidor version of Tolstoy's epic. *Audrey Hepburn*,
Henry Fonda and *John Mills* star. Spectacular battle scenes.

....

★★★ **The Wild One** 1954   79 mins (cert PG)
The original biker movie, which was once banned in Britain.
Misunderstood *Marlon Brando* and gang run riot in town.

....

★ **Wings of the Apache** 1990   89 mins (cert 15)
A poor man's 'Top Gun'. Helicopters instead of planes and
Nicolas Cage and *Sean Young* instead of Tom Cruise and Kelly
McGillis.

....

★★★ **The Wooden Horse** 1950   101 mins (cert U)
Solid British wartime escape drama with *Leo Genn* and *David
Tomlinson*.

....

★★★★ **The Young Lions** 1958   167 mins (cert PG)
A blond *Marlon Brando* takes some getting used to but this is a
gripping WWII story told from both the German and American
points of view.

....

★★ **You Only Live Twice** 1967   108 mins (cert PG)
Sean Connery in typical fast, jokey, James Bond caper. *Donald
Pleasence* as the evil Blofeld.

★★★★ **Zulu** 1964   133 mins (cert PG)
Stanley Baker and *Michael Caine* at Battle of Rourke's Drift during the Zulu wars. Superb battle scenes.

★★★ **Zulu Dawn** 1979   115 mins (cert PG)
A prequel to the above, with *Burt Lancaster* and *Peter O'Toole*, centring on the battle that immediately preceded Rourke's Drift.

COMEDY

★★ **Adventures in Babysitting** 1987   99 mins (cert 15)
Elizabeth Shue's babysitting stint goes crazily wrong on a wild
night out in Chicago. Amiable comedy/thriller.

★★ **The Adventures of Baron Munchausen** 1989   126 mins (cert PG)
Terry Gilliam's ambitious, uneven, sometimes dazzling tale of
the 18th-century Prussian fantasist (a rather miscast *John
Neville*). The parts are much better than the whole.

★★★ **After Hours** 1985   97 mins (cert 15)
Martin Scorsese's dark, funny comedy. Lonely *Griffin Dunne*'s
date with *Rosanna Arquette* turns into a nightmare in hostile
Manhattan.

★★★★ **Airplane!** 1980   98 mins (cert 12)
Hilarious skit on the 'Airport' disaster movies with *Leslie Nielsen*
and *Lloyd Bridges*.

★★★ **Airplane II: The Sequel** 1982   84 mins (cert 12)
Much the same as 'Airplane!', only not quite so good. Notable
cameo though from *William Shatner*, aka Captain Kirk.

★★★ **Alfie** 1966   114 mins (cert 15)
Dated but entertaining tale of philandering Cockney charmer
nicely played by *Michael Caine*.

★★★ **Alice** 1991   105 mins (cert 12)
Surreal moral comedy by Woody Allen. Rich, bored housewife
Mia Farrow finds the meaning of life from magical Chinese
herbs.

★★★ **All of Me** 1984   91 mins (cert 15)
Lily Tomlin shares *Steve Martin*'s body in screwball comedy with
a fair share of slapstick laughs.

★ **Almost an Angel** 1990   95 mins (cert PG)
Soppy, comic fable of soft-hearted crook given second chance at
life. Despite *Paul Hogan*, the jokes fall flat.

★★ **American Friends** 1991   95 mins (cert PG)
Michael Palin's gentle, affectionate re-telling of how his great
grandfather found true love.

★★★ **American Graffiti** 1973   110 mins (cert PG)
Director George Lucas' nostalgic look at 1960s USA. Great
rock 'n' roll soundtrack and impressive cast.

★★★ **And Now for Something
Completely Different** 1972   88 mins (cert PG)
Collection of Monty Python's TV best including that family
favourite 'The Dead Parrot' sketch.

★★★★ **Annie Hall** 1977   93 mins (cert 15)
Woody Allen's brilliant, Oscar-winning romantic comedy about a
neurotic Jewish comedian's troubled affair with a disorganised
WASP – *Diane Keaton* at her scattiest.

★ **Another You** 1991   94 mins (cert U)
Raucous comedy with *Gene Wilder*, as a mentally unstable
conman, put in the care of *Richard Pryor*'s street hustler. Neat
idea but that's as far as it goes. Fairly desperate stuff.

★★★★ **The Apartment** 1960   125 mins (cert PG)
Jack Lemmon and *Shirley MacLaine* shine in Billy Wilder's sharp
comedy/drama. An early, cynical exposé of inter-office
relationships.

★★★★ **Arsenic and Old Lace** 1944   118 mins (cert PG)
Cary Grant at his effortless best trying to stop two elderly ladies
poisoning lonely old men. Time-honoured classic that creaks
hardly at all in its old age.

★★★ **Arthur** 1981   97 mins (cert 15)
Dudley Moore as an alcoholic and unhappy millionaire risking his
inheritance for the woman he loves, *Liza Minnelli*. Daft but fun.
John Gielgud, as the butler, steals the show.

★ **Arthur II: On the Rocks** 1988   110 mins (cert PG)
Deeply feeble sequel in which Arthur does lose his inheritance
and strives to get it back.

★★ **Baby Boom** 1987   110 mins (cert PG)
Diane Keaton plays a yuppie who inherits a baby and finds
fulfilment. Charming and best of the baby movies that flooded
the screen around that time.

★★★ **Baby It's You** 1982   101 mins (cert 15)
Rosanna Arquette leads a neat cast in John Sayles' amusing look
at love and life in 1960s New Jersey.

★★★ **Bad Behaviour** 1993   100 mins (cert 15)
Comedy/drama about a London Irish household coping with all
manner of disasters. *Stephen Rea* and *Sinead Cusack* head a very
accomplished cast.

★★★ **Bananas** 1971   81 mins (cert 15)
Whacky, rather uneven caper from *Woody Allen* who finds
himself caught up in a South American revolution and becomes
a reluctant rebel leader. Fine sprinkling of splendid Allen gags.

★★★ **Barefoot in the Park** 1967   109 mins (cert PG)
Neil Simon's engaging play of struggling, squabbling,
Manhattan newly-weds, *Jane Fonda* and *Robert Redford*, coping
with in-laws, neighbours and the problems of a fifth-floor flat.

★★★ **Barton Fink** 1991   116 mins (cert 15)
Surreal comedy from the Coen Brothers about Hollywood,
writer's block and a serial killer. With *John Turturro* and *John
Goodman*.

★★★ **Beetlejuice** 1988   92 mins (cert 15)
Comic caper of ghosts, *Alec Baldwin* and *Geena Davis*, trying to
exorcise modernist family from home with help of whacky
Betelgeuse, *Michael Keaton*.

★★ **Betsy's Wedding** 1990   94 mins (cert 15)
Alan Alda's mannered comedy revolves around the preparations
for his daughter *Molly Ringwald*'s big day. Amiable but very
predictable.

★★ **The Big Picture** 1989   100 mins (cert 15)
Engaging satire with *Kevin Bacon* as a promising filmmaker
corrupted by Hollywood where integrity may (just) buy the
groceries but not the Porsche and the house in Beverly Hills.

★★★ **Biloxi Blues** 1988   100 mins (cert 15)
Neil Simon's delightful observations of the lives of raw recruits
in a wartime training camp. *Matthew Broderick* stars as the
innocent called to arms.

★★ **Bird on a Wire** 1990   111 mins (cert 12)
Acceptable action/comedy pairs ex-lovers, *Mel Gibson* and *Goldie
Hawn*, running from killers. The stars are better than the plot.

★ **Blame It on the Bellboy** 1992   79 mins (cert 12)
Weak and woolly comedy of errors as a hitman, an estate agent
and a blind-dater meet the wrong partners in Venice. *Dudley
Moore*, *Patsy Kensit* and *Richard Griffiths* among many famous
faces.

★★★★ **Blazing Saddles** 1974   93 mins (cert 15)
Mel Brooks' hilarious Western spoof with *Gene Wilder*. Notable
sequences include the celebrated farting scene after a bean
supper.

★★★ **Bob Roberts** 1992   104 mins (cert 15)
Tim Robbins wrote, directed, sang and starred in this clever
political satire as a hypocritical right-wing political candidate in
America. Numerous cameos and lovely support performance
from *Alan Rickman*.

★ **Boomerang** 1992   117 mins (cert 15)
Arrogant ladies' man *Eddie Murphy* overlooks nice *Halle Berry*
and gets his comeuppance at the hands of beautiful new boss,
Robin Givens. The odd good gag and Murphy appeals.

★ **Born Yesterday** 1993   101 mins (cert PG)
Don Johnson and *Melanie Griffith* helped in this 'Pygmalion'-style
comedy by the presence of *John Goodman*. But it's not a patch on
the 1950 original.

★★★★★ **Bringing Up Baby** 1938   102 mins (cert U)
Howard Hawkes' inspired, classic comedy. Marvellous pairing of
Cary Grant and *Katharine Hepburn* brought together by a missing
leopard.

★★★ **Broadcast News** 1987   127 mins (cert 15)
William Hurt, *Holly Hunter* and *Albert Brooks* in a sharp, funny
satire of the TV news industry.

★★★★ **Broadway Danny Rose** 1984   86 mins (cert PG)
Woody Allen as Broadway agent involved with third-rate variety
acts and Mafia moll, *Mia Farrow*. Delightful.

★★ **Cadillac Man** 1990   98 mins (cert 15)
Car salesman *Robin Williams* held hostage by *Tim Robbins* in a
comedy that starts well but fades fast.

★ **California Man** 1992   88 mins (cert PG)
Sean Astin unearths Neanderthal man in his back yard and
causes a comic stir when he takes him to school. Hopelessly
moronic stuff.

★★★★ **California Suite** 1978   103 mins (cert 15)
Four separate but intertwined stories of guests at the Beverly
Hills Hotel at Oscar time. Sharp, funny script by Neil Simon.
Great cast. *Maggie Smith* superb.

★★ **The Captain's Paradise** 1953   89 mins (cert U)
Polished comedy with *Alec Guinness* as British ferryboat captain
with wives in two ports.

★ **Carry On Columbus** 1992   91 mins (cert PG)
Latest and possibly worst of the 39 films in the series. Even a
reasonable cast can do little with the deeply naff script.

★★★ **Carry On Up the Khyber** 1968   88 mins (cert PG)
One of the best of series with typical lavatorial humour and
familiar, well-loved original cast. (Numerous other 'Carry On's
available on video have their moments but 'Carry On England'
is best avoided.)

★ **The Cat and the Canary** 1979   98 mins (cert 15)
Drab British remake of the old Bob Hope/Paulette Goddard
comedy/thriller. *Honor Blackman* does her best.

★★ **CB4** 1993   88 mins (cert 18)
Young, middle-class rappers enrage the hard man whose
identity they stole in so-so spoof on the rap scene.

★★ **A Chorus of Disapproval** 1988   99 mins (cert PG)
Michael Winner's movie adaptation of Alan Ayckbourn's
shrewd, funny play falls flat and wastes an excellent cast headed
by *Jeremy Irons* and *Anthony Hopkins*.

★★★ **City Lights** 1931   87 mins (cert U)
Charlie Chaplin's sweet but hugely sentimental classic about his
love for blind flower seller.

★★★ **City Slickers** 1991   114 mins (cert 12)
Witty, charming story in which *Billy Crystal*, *Bruno Kirby* and
Daniel Stern work out mid-life crisis on modern cattle drive.

★★★ **Clockwise** 1986   96 mins (cert PG)
Madcap vehicle for *John Cleese*, desperately trying to get to
Norwich in time for headmasters' convention.

★★ **Comfort and Joy** 1984   106 mins (cert PG)
Bill Forsyth's quirky story of ice cream wars in Glasgow. *Bill
Paterson* is splendid as disc jockey who inadvertently becomes
involved.

★★ **Company Business** 1991   98 mins (cert 15)
Three generations of a family attempt a robbery planned by
grandfather, *Sean Connery*. Even an excellent cast (*Dustin
Hoffman* and *Matthew Broderick* also star) can't make it work.

★★ **The Concierge** 1993   95 mins (cert PG)
Michael J Fox as the Mr Fix-It concierge of a Manhattan hotel
who can solve everyone's problems but his own. Fox makes the
script appear better than it is.

★★ **Cousins** 1989   113 mins (cert 15)
Ted Danson and *Isabella Rossellini* as lovers and cousins in family
comedy. Inferior American remake of French 'Cousin, Cousine'.

★★ **Crazy People** 1990   92 mins (cert 15)
Dudley Moore finds *Darryl Hannah* and sanity in a lunatic asylum.
Silly but sometimes agreeable.

★★★★ **Crimes and Misdemeanours** 1989   104 mins (cert 15)
Woody Allen's bold, skilful blending and bringing together of two
separate stories involving comedy, murder and adultery.

★★★ **Crossing Delancey** 1988   96 mins (cert PG)
Wistful tale with some charm of a romance and arranged
marriage in the Jewish community of downtown New York.

★★★ **Dancin' Thru the Dark** 1989   95 mins (cert 15)
Willy Russell's slice of Liverpudlian life. Hen night and stag
night converge on the same disco with disastrous results.

★★★ **Dave** 1993   110 mins (cert 12)
Kevin Kline impersonates president when incumbent has a
stroke but can he fool the nation, not to mention the first lady,
Sigourney Weaver? Very pleasing comedy with a tip or two to offer
any national leader.

★★★ **A Day at the Races** 1937   109 mins (cert U)
Typical *Marx Brothers* vehicle graced by *Maureen O'Hara*.
Perfunctory story; brothers on top form.

★★★ **Dead Men Don't Wear Plaid** 1982   88 mins (cert PG)
Clever editing sees private eye *Steve Martin* meeting late
Hollywood greats in pleasant film noir pastiche.

★ **Death Becomes Her** 1992   104 mins (cert PG)
Breathtaking special effects can't help the stupid plot. *Goldie
Hawn* and *Meryl Streep* find immortalizing drug – no matter
what harm befalls their bodies. *Bruce Willis* is the object of their
affections.

★★★★ **Desperately Seeking Susan** 1985   104 mins (cert 15)
Excellent comedy of mistaken identities between kooky *Rosanna
Arquette* and streetwise *Madonna* in her best film role to date.

★★★ **Dirty Rotten Scoundrels** 1988   110 mins (cert PG)
Good knockabout fun with *Steve Martin* and *Michael Caine* as
conmen working the French Riviera.

★★ **The Distinguished Gentleman** 1992   114 mins (cert 15)
Conman, *Eddie Murphy*, runs for congress and when there
quickly cleans up some of the shady deals in Washington. Funny
and romantic satire of American politics.

★★ **Don't Tell Her It's Me** 1990   102 mins (cert 12)
Shelley Long helps disfigured brother, *Steve Guttenberg*, win the
woman of his dreams in sloppy, vague comedy.

★★ **Down and Out in Beverly Hills** 1986   103 mins (cert 15)
Comic adventures prompted when tramp, *Nick Nolte*, tries to
commit suicide in *Richard Dreyfuss* and *Bette Midler*'s pool.

★★★ **Dragnet** 1987   106 mins (cert PG)
Amusing parody of TV police shows with *Tom Hanks* and *Dan
Aykroyd* as the hapless cops. Starts better than it finishes since
momentum tends to wane.

★★★ **The Dream Team** 1989   113 mins (cert 15)
Hilarious adventures of four mental patients – *Michael Keaton*,
Christopher Lloyd, *Peter Boyle* and *Stephen Furst* – at large in
downtown New York.

★★★★ **Dr Strangelove** 1964   93 mins (cert 15)
Triple role for *Peter Sellers* in Stanley Kubrick's deep black satire about crazy US General launching nuclear attack on Russia.

★ **Earth Girls Are Easy** 1989   100 mins (cert PG)
Vibrant colours and songs do little to help feeble comedy of three licentious aliens invading home of valley girl, *Geena Davis*.

★★ **Eat the Peach** 1986   95 mins (cert PG)
Engaging account of two unemployed Irish friends who decide to build a wall of death after seeing the Elvis movie 'Roustabout'.

★★ **18 Again!** 1988   100 mins (cert PG)
Aged *George Burns* and grandson, *Charlie Schlatter*, swap bodies with feeble results.

★★★ **Erik the Viking** 1989   102 mins (cert 12)
Monty Python's *Terry Jones* directed this scrappy, sometimes very funny, story of Norsemen setting off to save the world. Usual crew plus *Tim Robbins*.

★★★ **Everything You Always Wanted to Know About Sex** 1972   87 mins (cert 18)
Woody Allen's hotch-potch series of comic sketches. Very hit and miss. Sometimes you laugh, often you don't.

★★★ **Every Which Way But Loose** 1978   114 mins (cert 12)
Lightweight comedy with plenty of knockabout action pairing *Clint Eastwood* as gallant clod and an orang-utan as his smarter companion.

★★ **Father of the Bride** 1992   105 mins (cert PG)
Unnecessary remake of the Spencer Tracey/Elizabeth Taylor movie. *Steve Martin* too lightweight and too much the comedian to be convincing.

★★ **Filofax** 1990   108 mins (cert 12)
Convict, *James Belushi*, finds *Charles Grodin*'s filofax and takes over his life. Has its moments but not enough of them.

★★★ **The First Great Train Robbery** 1978   108 mins (cert 15)
Sean Connery stars enjoyably in Michael Crichton's Victorian caper about the first and hitherto little-known theft from a moving train.

★★★★ **A Fish Called Wanda** 1988   108 mins (cert 15)
Hilarious romantic caper. *John Cleese* and *Jamie Lee Curtis* as
barrister and crook in love. *Kevin Kline* steals the movie as her
dim, jealous suitor.

★ **Folks** 1992   102 mins (cert PG)
Tom Selleck loses bits of his anatomy as he cares for his senile
father, *Don Ameche*, in a desperate comedy that attempts,
fatally, to deal with Alzheimer's Disease.

★★★ **The Fortune Cookie** 1966   125 mins (cert U)
Substandard Billy Wilder comedy in which *Jack Lemmon* and
Walter Matthau try to pull off an insurance scam.

★★ **Foul Play** 1978   116 mins (cert PG)
Detective *Chevy Chase* falls in love with suspect *Goldie Hawn*,
unwittingly involved in a plot to kill the Pope. *Dudley Moore* also
involved.

★ **Frauds** 1992   90 mins (cert 15)
Phil Collins in thin black comedy investigates an insurance fraud
and blackmails the culprits until they fight back. Bit frenetic.

★★★★ **The Freshman** 1990   103 mins (cert PG)
College student, *Matthew Broderick*, falls in with mobster, *Marlon
Brando*, here gloriously parodying his 'Godfather' role. A very
funny and offbeat comedy.

★★ **Frozen Assets** 1993   95 mins (cert 12)
Romantic cryogenics comedy. Manager of sperm bank ensures a
plentiful supply by running an outrageous virility contest. With
Shelley Long and *Corbin Bernsen*.

★★★★ **The General** 1927   80 mins (cert U)
The best of *Buster Keaton*'s stunt-filled romps, set during the
American Civil War. Keaton in search of his stolen train – and
his sweetheart.

★★★ **Gentlemen Prefer Blondes** 1953   91 mins (cert U)
Howard Hawkes' musical comedy provides lightweight but
agreeable show-case for man-hungry *Marilyn Monroe* and *Jane
Russell*.

★★ **Georgy Girl** 1966   100 mins (cert 18)
Frumpy *Lynn Redgrave* is mistress to *James Mason* with *Charlotte Rampling* as her bitchy friend in swinging Sixties comedy.

★★★ **Ghengis Cohn** 1993   111 mins (cert PG)
Jewish comedian *Anthony Sher*, killed at Auschwitz, returns to haunt SS officers and convert them to Judaism. *Robert Lindsay* as the chief-of-police learning to love kosher food.

★★★★ **Ghost** 1990   126 mins (cert 12)
Hugely popular comedy/drama sees murdered *Patrick Swayze* returning to protect his threatened lover, *Demi Moore*. *Whoopi Goldberg* as medium lifts tone delightfully.

★★ **The Gods Must Be Crazy** 1981   108 mins (cert 15)
Three stories amalgamate in eccentric slapstick from South Africa which has developed cult following.

★★★★★ **The Gold Rush** 1925   72 mins (cert U)
The Klondike 1898 provides the setting for *Charlie Chaplin*'s silent classic in which he eats his footwear.

★★★ **The Goodbye Girl** 1977   110 mins (cert PG)
Touching, funny, love story involving lodger, *Richard Dreyfuss*, and divorcee, *Marsha Mason*. Written adeptly by Neil Simon.

★★★ **Good Morning Vietnam** 1987   121 mins (cert 15)
Fine performance by *Robin Williams* as irreverent DJ cheering the troops in Vietnam.

★★★ **Green Card** 1990   107 mins (cert 12)
Romantic comedy featuring *Gerard Depardieu* and *Andie MacDowell* in a marriage of convenience and a divorce of courtship.

★★★★★ **Gregory's Girl** 1980   91 mins (cert PG)
Superb direction by Bill Forsyth and an outstanding debut by *John Gordon Sinclair*. A comic jewel that should appear in anyone's top ten favourites.

★★★★ **Groundhog Day** 1993   103 mins (cert PG)
Bill Murray finds himself living the same day over and over and over again – until he gets it right. Very funny and thought-provoking.

★★★★ **Guess Who's Coming to Dinner** 1967   112 mins (cert PG)
Spencer Tracy and *Katharine Hepburn* forced to come to terms with inter-racial marriage of daughter *Katharine Houghton* to *Sidney Poitier*. Tracy's last film.

★★ **Hairspray** 1988   88 mins (cert PG)
John Waters' nostalgic, comic satire of the style and fashions of the dance-crazed 1960s.

★★★ **Hannah and Her Sisters** 1986   107 mins (cert 15)
Woody Allen's best plot to date concentrates on the fortunes of three sisters – *Mia Farrow*, *Barbara Hershey* and *Dianne Wiest*. Oscar for *Michael Caine*, who also stars.

★ **Happy Together** 1989   96 mins (cert U)
Enthusiastic performances by *Patrick Dempsey* and *Helen Slater* rescue teenage romance plot from banality. Just.

★★★★ **Harvey** 1950   104 mins (cert U)
Sheer delight about an endearing drunk, *James Stewart*, whose relatives want him committed due to his friendship with a six-foot, invisible rabbit called Harvey.

★★★★ **Hear My Song** 1991   103 mins (cert 15)
Delightful, heart-warming tale of nightclub owner trying to find noted, tax-dodging Irish tenor Josef Locke and bring him to Liverpool for a concert. *Adrian Dunbar* and *Ned Beatty* excel.

★★ **The Heartbreak Kid** 1972   106 mins (cert PG)
Charles Grodin tires of wife on honeymoon where he falls for *Cybill Shepherd* in poignant, bitter-sweet Neil Simon comedy of embarrassment.

★★ **Heart Condition** 1990   100 mins (cert 15)
Racist cop, *Bob Hoskins*, given heart of dead black lawyer, *Denzel Washington*, who returns to haunt him, help him and change him.

★★ **High Anxiety** 1977   94 mins (cert 15)
Disappointing, sporadically funny attempt by *Mel Brooks* to do to Hitchcock what he'd done to the Western in 'Blazing Saddles'.

★★★ **High Hopes** 1988   110 mins (cert 15)
Mike Leigh's biting condemnation of Thatcherite London, yuppiedom and the like. A strong ensemble cast extracts the full humour and satire from the sharp dialogue.

★★★ **Honeymoon in Vegas** 1993   95 mins (cert 12)
Nicolas Cage loses fiancée, *Sarah Jessica Parker*, in card game to wealthy *James Caan*. Best and funniest of the crop of films treating women as commodities. Lovely running gag about Elvis impersonators.

★★★★ **Hope and Glory** 1987   113 mins (cert 15)
John Boorman's delightful, nostalgic and autobiographical story of life as a small boy during WWII.

★★★ **Hot Shots** 1991   85 mins (cert 12)
Charlie Sheen and *Lloyd Bridges* attempt to do to 'Top Gun' what 'Airplane!' did to 'Airport'. Nice try, doesn't quite work; the sequel gets nearer the mark.

★★★ **Hot Shots Part Deux** 1992   89 mins (cert 12)
'Rambo' spoof, though many more films come in for the typical treatment. *Charlie Sheen* and *Lloyd Bridges* funnier than before.

★★★ **Housesitter** 1992   102 mins (cert PG)
Frenetic comedy in which *Goldie Hawn* poses as *Steve Martin*'s wife after a one-night stand with him. Moving into his unoccupied new home she becomes the bane of his life. Hawn overly kooky and Martin's talents stifled.

★★ **How to Get Ahead in Advertising** 1989   104 mins (cert 15)
More satirical than funny comedy about marketing man, *Richard E Grant*, with a talking boil on his neck.

★★★ **Husbands and Wives** 1992   108 mins (cert 15)
Marital strife as *Sydney Pollack* and *Judy Davis* announce their separation leaving other couple, *Woody Allen* and *Mia Farrow*, to re-examine the shaky foundations of their own marriage.

★★ **I Love You to Death** 1990   98 mins (cert 15)
True, comic story about a wife, *Tracy Ullman*, who botched numerous attempts to murder her cheating husband, *Kevin Kline*. *River Phoenix*, *William Hurt* and *Joan Plowright* also star.

★★★ **I'm Alright Jack** 1959   104 mins (cert U)
Funny spoof on the British work ethic. *Peter Sellers* and *Ian Carmichael* head excellent cast.

★★★★ **I'm Gonna Git You, Sucka** 1988   89 mins (cert 15)
Hip, witty parody of 1970s blaxploitation movies, written and directed by its star *Keenen Ivory Wayans*.

★★★ **The Importance of Being Ernest** 1952   95 mins (cert U)
Edith Evans' delivery of the line 'A handbag' immortalized this delightful adaptation of Oscar Wilde's comic play.

★★ **Indiscreet** 1958   100 mins (cert PG)
Typically enjoyable *Cary Grant* romantic comedy. *Ingrid Bergman* as the woman he can't forget.

★★ **Innocent Blood** 1993   113 mins (cert 15)
Vampire story with a difference. *Anne Parillaud* is the fanged predator, fancying Italian and biting into neck of Mob boss, *Robert Loggia*. Biting off more than she can chew in funny, rather quirky, bloodbath.

★★★★★ **It Happened One Night** 1934   105 mins (cert U)
Frank Capra's glorious romantic comedy. Marvellous pairing of reporter *Clark Gable* and runaway heiress *Claudette Colbert* won all the major Oscars that year.

★★ **Jabberwocky** 1977   110 mins (cert PG)
Terry Gilliam's hit-and-miss medieval romp about serfs and a dragon. *Michael Palin* stars.

★★★★ **The Jerk** 1979   94 mins (cert 15)
Steve Martin in first leading role as naive white boy leaving his adoptive black family and joining a circus. Hilarious.

★★ **Joe Versus the Volcano** 1990   102 mins (cert PG)
Lightweight but very enjoyable fantasy about a hypochondriac, *Tom Hanks*, conned into making himself a human sacrifice. *Meg Ryan* provides an amusing diversion in three different roles.

★★ **Just Like a Woman** 1992   106 mins (cert 15)
Divorcee *Julie Walters* falls in love with lodger, *Adrian Pasdar*, only to discover he's a transvestite. Not so much a comedy, more a poignant tale of small lives not conforming to the norm.

★★ **Just One of the Girls** 1992   98 mins (cert 15)
Corey Haim poses as female to avoid classroom bully but falls in love with the girl who befriends him – a far cry from 'Tootsie', I fear.

★★★ **Kentucky Fried Movie** 1977   104 mins (cert 18)
Irreverent series of skits and sketches from the creators of 'Airplane!' Vulgar, hilarious, and often both.

★★★★★ **Kind Hearts and Coronets** 1949   106 mins (cert U)
Marvellous Ealing black comedy in which *Alec Guinness* plays all eight members of an aristocratic family murdered by title-hunting *Dennis Price*.

★★ **King Ralph** 1991   95 mins (cert PG)
Daft, witless farce has Las Vegas cabaret artist, *John Goodman*, ascending to British throne.

★★★★ **The Ladykillers** 1955   97 mins (cert U)
Ealing caper of highest class. Gang of crooks, *Alec Guinness*, *Peter Sellers*, et al, thwarted by a sweet little old lady, beautifully played by *Katie Johnson*.

★★★ **LA Story** 1990   95 mins (cert 15)
Amiable *Steve Martin* comedy about love and life in smog-ridden city. Some, but not enough, excellent moments.

★★★★ **The Lavender Hill Mob** 1951   78 mins (cert U)
Classic Ealing stuff. *Alec Guinness* plans the perfect robbery, aided and abetted by *Stanley Holloway* and *Sid James*.

★★★★ **A League of Their Own** 1992   128 mins (cert PG)
Very funny look at women's baseball in WWII. *Geena Davis* is excellent as the star player, *Tom Hanks* equally good as her team's drunken manager. *Madonna* not bad either.

★★ **Leap of Faith** 1992   108 mins (cert PG)
Curious *Steve Martin* vehicle in which he plays a bogus travelling evangelist whose troupe fetches up, with unexpected results, in a small American town. At its best when Martin's doing his stuff.

★★★ **Lenny: Live and Unleashed** 1989   94 mins (cert 15)
Lenny Henry's one-man show. Very funny in parts, particularly his brilliant take-off of Steve Martin.

★★ **Leon the Pig Farmer** 1992   104 mins (cert 15)
Emotional chaos ensues when a Jewish boy, *Mark Frankel*, discovers his real father's a Yorkshire pork farmer. *Brian Glover*, *Connie Booth*, *Janet Suzman* and *Gina Bellman* complete the cast of an engaging low-budget movie.

★★★ **Letter to Brezhnev** 1985   94 mins (cert 15)
Likeable Liverpudlian comedy about two girls, *Alexandra Pigg* and *Margi Clark*, seeking aid of Soviet president in their romance with Russian soldiers.

★★★★ **Life Is Sweet** 1990   102 mins (cert 15)
So is this smashing, funny delight from Mike Leigh. A slice of
suburban family life which is not to be missed. *Jane Horrocks*
shines as the bulimic daughter of the household.

....

★ **Life Stinks** 1991   95 mins (cert 12)
As does this feeble, patronising effort by *Mel Brooks*, who stars as
a ruthless millionaire forced to experience life as a tramp.

....

★★ **Like Father Like Son** 1987   98 mins (cert PG)
Dudley Moore's contribution to the life-swap movies that
proliferated around this time. He changes places with his
16-year-old son, *Kirk Cameron*, in an engaging enough tale.

....

★★★ **The Little Shop of Horrors** 1986   94 mins (cert PG)
Mixed genres of horror, comedy and music spark mixed
reactions to Frank Oz's movie. *Rick Moranis*, *Steve Martin* and
Bill Murray among the cast.

....

★★★★ **Look Who's Talking** 1989   96 mins (cert 12)
Original comedy of a baby's eye-view of the world (voiced by
Bruce Willis). *Kirstie Alley* as single mother, *John Travolta* the cab-
driving baby-sitter and *George Segal* the father.

....

★ **Look Who's Talking Too** 1990   81 mins (cert 12)
Baby Mikey gets a sister (voiced by *Roseanne Barr*) in witless,
uncharming sequel.

....

★★★ **Love and Death** 1975   85 mins (cert PG)
One of *Woody Allen*'s best. Sharp skit on Russian literature and
various movies. *Diane Keaton* co-stars.

....

★★ **Love at First Bite** 1979   96 mins (cert 15)
Pleasing spoof of Dracula movies with *George Hamilton* as suave
20th-century Count with a lust for blood and *Susan Saint James*
his happy victim.

....

★★ **Made in America** 1993   111 mins (cert 12)
Whoopi Goldberg finds the surrogate father of her daughter is a
white, second-hand car salesman, *Ted Danson*. Frenetic, fairly
funny comedy of errors.

....

★ **Madhouse** 1990   90 mins (cert 15)
Silly family farce, full of racial and sexual stereotypes, about guests
who never leave. Redeemed somewhat by presence of *Kirstie Alley*.

★ **The Maid** 1991   101 mins (cert 12)
Businessman, *Martin Sheen*, becomes *Jacqueline Bisset*'s maid in order to woo her. Lightweight romantic comedy.

....

★★★★ **Manhattan** 1979   96 mins (cert 15)
Woody Allen's satirical black-and-white comedy of life and love in his beloved New York. *Diane Keaton* and *Mariel Hemingway* are the objects of Allen's desire.

....

★★★ **The Man in the White Suit** 1951   85 mins (cert U)
Alec Guinness as scientist who's invented everlasting cloth. Big business wants formula destroyed in delightful Ealing comedy.

....

★ **Man Trouble** 1992   100 mins (cert 15)
Silly slapstick as *Ellen Barkin* hires a guard dog from trainer, *Jack Nicholson*, and both become embroiled in chase to find her kidnapped sister. Pretty wide of the humorous mark.

....

★★★★★ **The Man with Two Brains** 1983   93 mins (cert 15)
Steve Martin's funniest comedy. He plays a brilliant brain surgeon seduced by conniving vamp, *Kathleen Turner*.

....

★★ **Matinee** 1992   99 mins (cert PG)
Better film within film than it is film. *John Goodman* is fine as a Sixties schlock horror movie king in a very uneven comedy.

....

★★ **Meet the Feebles** 1992   92 mins (cert 18)
Vulgar, violent and vaguely amusing animated feature of life in a puppet theatre. And the goings on are nobody's business.

....

★★ **Memoirs of an Invisible Man** 1992   99 mins (cert PG)
Decidedly soppy comedy remake by John Carpenter of the Claude Rains classic with *Chevy Chase* in the title role, *Darryl Hannah* as the love interest.

....

★★★★ **Mermaids** 1990   111 mins (cert 15)
Terrific romantic comedy featuring *Cher* as the single mother unable to settle down, *Winona Ryder* her troublesome daughter, and *Bob Hoskins* the new man in her life. Great swinging Sixties soundtrack.

....

★★ **Metropolitan** 1990   98 mins (cert 15)
Sharply original comedy that neatly satirizes the world of young, uppercrust New York yuppies.

★★ **Micki + Maude** 1984   118 mins (cert PG)
Dudley Moore amusing as bigamist trying to placate his two wives, *Amy Irving* and *Ann Reinking*.

....

★★★ **Midnight Run** 1988   126 mins (cert 15)
Comedy/action/adventure matches bounty hunter *Robert De Niro* against fugitive *Charles Grodin*, whose performance steals the film.

....

★★★ **Midnight Sting** 1992   98 mins (cert 15)
Conman *James Woods*, released from prison, heads for a town ruled by *Bruce Dern* to carry out a boxing scam involving *Louis Gossett Jr*. Clever and nicely entertaining.

....

★★★ **A Midsummer Night's Sex Comedy** 1982   98 mins (cert 15)
Woody Allen's wryly amusing look at sexual interaction of three couples on a weekend holiday.

....

★★ **The Missionary** 1982   86 mins (cert 15)
Easy-going comedy with *Michael Palin* as minister helping fallen women in Victorian London.

....

★★★★ **Monty Python and the Holy Grail** 1973   90 mins (cert 15)
Comic crew's wickedly funny send-up of the Arthurian legend. A kind of very upmarket 'Carry On Arthur'.

....

★★★★ **Monty Python's Life of Brian** 1979   93 mins (cert 15)
Hugely controversial and achingly funny send-up of organised religion in which Brian is mistaken for the Messiah. Easily the best of all the Python movies.

....

★★ **Monty Python's The Meaning of Life** 1983   90 mins (cert 15)
Monty Python's irreverent, uneven series of sketches exploring various facets of life and death. Occasionally hilarious but not often enough.

....

★★ **Mr Baseball** 1993   104 mins (cert 15)
Tom Selleck past his sell-by-date on the pitch, transferred to Japanese team. Comic look at the personality and cultural clashes.

....

★★★★ **Mr Deeds Goes to Town** 1936   118 mins (cert U)
Frank Capra's immaculate social comedy wherein *Gary Cooper* inherits a fortune and finds his sanity disputed when he tries to give it away.

★★ **Mr Saturday Night** 1992   119 mins (cert 15)
Billy Crystal's rather depressing comedy about the life of a
comedian and his brother through the rise and fall of their act.
Neither ages convincingly – the make-up just gets heavier and
whiter.

★★★ **Mrs Doubtfire** 1993   121 mins (cert 12)
Divorced *Robin Williams* disguises himself as a nanny to be near
his children. As a woman he's fine; as a man he's far too
sentimental. *Pierce Brosnan* nearly steals the film.

★★★ **Mr Wonderful** 1993   98 mins (cert 15)
Matt Dillon wants to rid himself of alimony payments so tries to
fix up ex-wife, *Anabella Sciorra*, with a husband. Truly romantic
by 'Truly, Madly, Deeply' director, Anthony Minghella.

★★★★ **Much Ado About Nothing** 1993   110 mins (cert 15)
Glorious and most accessible adaptation of Shakespeare's
comedy with *Emma Thompson* and director *Kenneth Branagh* as
Beatrice and Benedick, ably supported by *Denzel Washington*,
Keanu Reeves, *Michael Keaton* and *Richard Briers*.

★★ **Murder by Death** 1976   94 mins (cert PG)
Neil Simon's spoof of murder mysteries provides passable comic
vehicle for *Peter Sellers*, *Maggie Smith* and *David Niven*.

★★★ **My Blue Heaven** 1990   96 mins (cert PG)
Sometimes very funny story of a mobster, *Steve Martin*, who goes
into the witness protection programme with the help of FBI
agent *Rick Moranis*.

★★ **My Cousin Vinny** 1992   119 mins (cert 15)
Courtroom comedy with *Joe Pesci* as inept lawyer defending
cousin, *Ralph Macchio*, on murder charge. Good start, good end,
flabby in the middle.

★★★★ **My Favourite Year** 1982   92 mins (cert PG)
Peter O'Toole walks off with this funny, touching tale of a boozy,
has-been actor – a kind of washed-up Errol Flynn – making his
come-back on a live TV show.

★★ **My Stepmother Is an Alien** 1988   107 mins (cert 15)
Scientist *Dan Aykroyd* involved in comic capers when he marries
extra-terrestrial, *Kim Basinger*. Has its moments.

★★★★ **Naked** 1993   126 mins (cert 18)
Mike Leigh's blackest comedy to date examines the brutishness
of modern Britain with savage humour. *David Thewlis'*
performance is a tour-de-force.

....

★★★★ **The Naked Gun** 1988   85 mins (cert 15)
Hilarious police spoof starring *Leslie Nielsen* and *Priscilla Presley*,
who proves herself a surprisingly good comedienne. By the
makers of 'Airplane!'

....

★★★ **The Naked Gun 2½** 1991   81 mins (cert 12)
Nearly as funny as original. *Leslie Nielsen's* back to save the
world from toxic waste, aided and abetted by *Priscilla Presley.*

....

★★★★ **Nashville** 1975   159 mins (cert PG)
Robert Altman's sly, witty comedy/drama which brings a score
of disparate characters together at a country music concert.
Great stuff.

....

★★ **The National Health** 1973   97 mins (cert U)
Jim Dale and *Lynn Redgrave* star in acerbic black comedy about
the British health service.

....

★★★ **National Lampoon's Animal House** 1978   104 mins (cert 15)
Sex, drugs and rock 'n' roll are the targets of a hit-and-miss
American college farce with *John Belushi* at his grossest and
probably funniest. First of the National Lampoon series.

....

★★ **National Lampoon's Christmas Vacation** 1989   97 mins (cert PG)
Chevy Chase and *Beverly D'Angelo* on their third holiday – this
time spent at home. Uninvited relations cause havoc as they
pop in during the festive season.

....

★★ **National Lampoon's European Vacation** 1985   94 mins (cert 15)
The Griswolds descend on Europe and England with frenetic
results. Hit-and-miss comedy, though *Eric Idle* scores a bullseye
as polite British cyclist.

....

★★ **National Lampoon's Loaded Weapon** 1993   83 mins (cert PG)
Emilio Estevez and *Samuel Jackson* in a send-up of the 'Lethal
Weapon' movies. Some of it's not bad but the mickey-taking
formula is fast running out of steam.

★★★ **National Lampoon's Vacation** 1983 98 mins (cert 15)
First and best of the series about the hapless Griswold, *Chevy Chase*, and his unfortunate wife, *Beverly D'Angelo*. Amusing fiasco of a holiday as they travel across America en famille.

★★★★ **A Night at the Opera** 1935 90 mins (cert U)
Possibly the best-loved film from the *Marx Brothers*, though 'Duck Soup' is better.

★★★ **9 to 5** 1980 110 mins (cert 15)
Cast – *Jane Fonda*, *Lily Tomlin* and *Dolly Parton* – better than plot in office-based satire. Has its moments though.

★★★★★ **Ninotchka** 1939 110 mins (cert U)
Greta Garbo's most joyous performance as hard-nosed Russian envoy succumbing to love and the lure of capitalism.

★★ **Noises Off** 1991 104 mins (cert 15)
Amusing backstage farce featuring a touring thespian company including *Michael Caine*, *Denholm Elliott*, *Christopher Reeve* and *Marilu Henner*.

★★★ **Nuns on the Run** 1990 95 mins (cert 12)
Pleasing British farce with *Robbie Coltrane* and *Eric Idle* posing as nuns to avoid hitmen.

★★★★ **Nuts in May** 1984 100 mins (cert 12)
Hilarious, slice-of-life comedy by Mike Leigh about a right-on, 'green' couple taking a camping holiday.

★★★★ **The Odd Couple** 1968 105 mins (cert 12)
Jack Lemmon and *Walter Matthau* are splendidly funny as two incompatible men sharing a flat in Neil Simon's comedy.

★★★ **One, Two, Three** 1961 115 mins (cert U)
An American executive in West Berlin is in trouble when boss's daughter marries Communist. Billy Wilder comedy; *James Cagney*'s last starring role.

★ **Only the Lonely** 1991 104 mins (cert 12)
Thin comedy about shy policeman, *John Candy*, falling for an undertaker's daughter, *Alley Sheedy*, despite mother *Maureen O'Hara*'s disapproval.

★★ **Oscar** 1991   110 mins (cert PG)
Farcical plot revolving around marriage plans of mafiosa boss's
daughter. *Sylvester Stallone* reveals surprisingly light touch.
Rather sweet if you like that sort of thing.

★★ **Other People's Money** 1991   101 mins (cert 15)
Ruthless Wall Street tycoon, *Danny DeVito*, defied by
honourable, old-fashioned *Gregory Peck*. Fast and amusing.

★★★ **Outrageous Fortune** 1987   100 mins (cert 15)
Ill-matched *Bette Midler* and *Shelley Long* join forces to find the
man who deceived them both, in agreeable, raucous adventure.

★★ **Overboard** 1987   112 mins (cert PG)
Amnesia causes bitchy heiress, *Goldie Hawn*, to rough it as
housekeeper to *Kurt Russell* and his kids in light romantic
comedy.

★★ **The Owl and the Pussycat** 1970   96 mins (cert 18)
Barbra Streisand and *George Segal* charm as incongruous couple –
she a prostitute, he a learned bookkeeper.

★★★ **Parenthood** 1989   124 mins (cert 12)
Touching, funny insights into problems of parenthood in one
large family. *Steve Martin* heads splendid cast.

★★★★ **Passport to Pimlico** 1949   84 mins (cert U)
Wonderful Ealing comedy in which a London borough declares
independence when an ancient Royal Charter is unearthed.

★★ **Peggy Sue Got Married** 1986   103 mins (cert 15)
'Back to the Future' yarn. Disillusioned *Kathleen Turner* given
chance to return to high school and change her life.

★★ **Personal Services** 1987   105 mins (cert 18)
Exploits of notorious London brothel-keeper, Cynthia Payne,
played by *Julie Walters*. Nice study of British sexual mores.

★★ **Peter's Friends** 1992   101 mins (cert 15)
Similar to 'The Big Chill' since it involves reunion of old college
friends some years down the line. Alternately amusing and
touching. *Kenneth Branagh* stars and directs a strong cast.

★★★ **The Pink Panther** 1964   113 mins (cert 15)
David Niven, the suave cat-burglar pursued by bungling sûreté Inspector Clouseau. *Peter Sellers* is hilarious in his first outing as the inept copper.

....

★★★ **The Pink Panther Strikes Again** 1976   103 mins (cert U)
The fifth of the Panther films – *Sellers*, *Herbert Lom*, *Burt Kwouk*, et al, in the search for a kidnapped scientist.

....

★ **Planes, Trains and Automobiles** 1987   93 mins (cert 15)
Surprisingly unfunny comedy of problems encountered by *Steve Martin* trying to get home for Thanksgiving. *John Candy* does little to help.

....

★★★★ **The Player** 1992   124 mins (cert 15)
Marvellously witty satire on Hollywood as big-shot script commissioner, *Tim Robbins*, becomes embroiled in murder. Count the cameo appearances – more than 60 of them.

....

★★★ **Play It Again, Sam** 1972   86 mins (cert 15)
Woody Allen on top form as writer coached by ghost of *Humphrey Bogart* in efforts to win *Diane Keaton* – some clever editing employed.

....

★★★ **Plaza Suite** 1971   114 mins (cert PG)
Three funny Neil Simon playlets all linked by same suite in New York's Plaza Hotel.

....

★ **The Pleasure Principle** 1992   96 mins (cert 18)
Divorcee *Peter Firth* juggles complex relationships with three women – *Haydn Gwynne*, *Lysette Anthony* and *Lynsey Baxter*. Funnyish.

....

★★ **Police Academy** 1984   95 mins (cert 18)
Farcical romp set in police training camp where misfit recruits need licking into shape. Six sequels reprise the gags less effectively.

....

★★ **The Pope Must Die** 1991   97 mins (cert 15)
Up-and-down comedy of errors. *Robbie Coltrane* is mistakenly appointed head of the Vatican.

....

★★ **The Pope of Greenwich Village** 1984   120 mins (cert 15)
Sharply observed study of New York hustler, *Mickey Rourke*, reluctantly involved with cousin, *Eric Roberts*, in mad schemes.

★ **Porky's** 1981   95 mins (cert 18)
Teenage hormones create havoc in 1950s school camp, but
rarely raise a laugh. Was popular enough to lead to two dumb
sequels.

★★★★ **Pretty Woman** 1990   120 mins (cert 15)
Irresistible fairytale of hooker, *Julia Roberts*, falling in love with
wealthy businessman client, *Richard Gere*.

★★★ **The Prime of Miss Jean Brodie** 1969   116 mins (cert 15)
Maggie Smith as avant-garde schoolmistress steering her charges
towards womanhood is both funny and touching.

★★★ **A Private Function** 1985   94 mins (cert 15)
Funny, sometimes cruel, comedy set in food-rationed, post-war
England with *Michael Palin* and *Maggie Smith*.

★★★ **The Private Life of Sherlock Holmes** 1970   125 mins (cert PG)
Billy Wilder's affectionate look at hitherto unknown aspects of
the great detective's career. With *Robert Stevens* and *Colin
Blakely*.

★★★ **Private's Progress** 1956   102 mins (cert U)
Good humoured army farce with *Ian Carmichael*, the national
serviceman duped by thieves. *Terry-Thomas* and *Richard
Attenborough* in support.

★★ **Pump Up the Volume** 1990   102 mins (cert 15)
Teenage movie with *Christian Slater* a high school kid by day, a
pirate radio DJ by night.

★★ **Punchline** 1988   122 mins (cert 15)
Oddly glum tale about comedy. Stand-up comic, *Tom Hanks*,
teaches housewife, *Sally Field*, how to make people laugh.

★★★★ **The Purple Rose of Cairo** 1985   82 mins (cert PG)
Delightful Woody Allen comedy with *Mia Farrow* as down-
trodden housewife whose hero, *Jeff Daniels*, steps out of movie
screen and sweeps her away.

★★ **The Queen of Hearts** 1990   112 mins (cert PG)
Italian family running cafe in London find things don't go as
smoothly as planned. Whimsical story combining comedy,
romance and magic with not quite enough of any.

★★★ **Quick Change** 1990   89 mins (cert 15)
The bank raid's easy. It's the getting out of NY that proves tricky for *Bill Murray* and gang. Appealing and funny.

★★★ **Radio Days** 1987   85 mins (cert PG)
Woody Allen's nostalgic, always amusing, reminiscences of boyhood in 1950s Queens, New York.

★★★★ **Raining Stones** 1993   90 mins (cert 15)
Blistering Ken Loach satire on life in recession-hit North of England. It should make you laugh and make you angry. Excellent performances do justice to fine script.

★★ **Raising Arizona** 1987   94 mins (cert 15)
Childless couple, *Nicolas Cage* and *Holly Hunter*, plan to steal one of quintuplets. Untidy comedy. Pre-credit sequence the best.

★★ **Rebecca's Daughters** 1992   90 mins (cert 12)
19th-century Welsh revolt against English toll gates when the men dressed as women. Degenerates into farce but worth watching for the energetic performance from *Peter O'Toole* who looks like Elizabeth I.

★★ **Repo Man** 1984   92 mins (cert 18)
Veteran car-repossessor *Harry Dean Stanton* shows rookie *Emilio Estevez* how to do it. Offbeat satire.

★ **Repossessed** 1990   85 mins (cert 15)
Hit-and-miss spoof of 'The Exorcist' with *Leslie Nielsen* driving out the devil. *Linda Blair* reprising her original role, but now a head-revolving, projectile-vomiting housewife.

★★ **Reuben, Reuben** 1983   101 mins (cert 15)
Anarchic comedy of dissolute writer, *Tom Conti*, sponging off married women until he meets beautiful nurse, *Kelly McGillis*.

★★★ **Richard Pryor Live in Concert** 1982   78 mins (cert 18)
Some achingly funny – and very rude – stuff taken from the comic's stand-up show.

★★★ **Riff-Raff** 1991   95 mins (cert 15)
Ken Loach's funny, biting satire of Britain under the Tories. Set on a building site.

★★★ **Risky Business** 1983　　　　　　　98 mins　(cert 18)
Teenager *Tom Cruise* turns his absent parents' home into a
brothel in an imaginative coming-of-age comedy.

★ **Robin Hood: Men in Tights** 1993　　　105 mins　(cert U)
Mel Brooks' disappointing send up of Kevin Costner's 'Robin
Hood: Prince of Thieves'. Why send up what wasn't a very good
film in the first place?

★★★ **The Rocky Horror Picture Show** 1975　　95 mins　(cert 15)
An innocent couple take refuge in a house packed with weirdos
in this camp but funny send-up of horror pix. *Tim Curry* and
Susan Sarandon lead.

★★ **Room Service** 1938　　　　　　　78 mins　(cert U)
Marx Brothers as destitute producers holed up in a hotel room.
Okay but not one of their best.

★★ **Rosencrantz and Guildenstern Are Dead** 1990　　117 mins　(cert PG)
Tom Stoppard directs lively screen version of his own play. *Tim
Roth* and *Gary Oldman* as hapless, untrustworthy and ill-fated
friends.

★★★ **Roxanne** 1987　　　　　　　107 mins　(cert PG)
Steve Martin's funny, modern-day version of 'Cyrano de Bergerac'
set around a fire station. *Darryl Hannah* is the latter-day Roxanne.

★★★ **Ruthless People** 1986　　　　　　94 mins　(cert 18)
Bette Midler is so spoiled that when she's kidnapped, husband
Danny DeVito refuses to pay the ransom. Great comic
performance by Midler.

★★ **Sabrina Fair** 1954　　　　　　　113 mins　(cert U)
So-so romantic comedy from Billy Wilder with a miscast
Humphrey Bogart falling for chauffeur's daughter, *Audrey Hepburn*.

★★ **Scenes from a Mall** 1991　　　　　88 mins　(cert 15)
Disappointing Paul Mazursky comedy starring *Woody Allen* in
which an anniversary shopping trip brings out startling marital
revelations between Allen and wife, *Bette Midler*.

★★ **Scrooged** 1988　　　　　　　101 mins　(cert PG)
Contemporary, comic version of Dickens' 'A Christmas Carol'.
Bill Murray finds festive spirit with the help of three hip ghosts.
Not great, not terrible.

★★★ **The Secret Life of Walter Mitty** 1947   110 mins (cert U)
Whimsical charmer with *Danny Kaye* as the timid Mitty – based
on James Thurber character – who daydreams of being a hero.
Virginia Mayo as love interest.

★★ **See No Evil, Hear No Evil** 1990   107 mins (cert 15)
Silly comedy in which a blind *Richard Pryor* and deaf *Gene Wilder*
get together to clear up the murder of which they're wrongly
suspected.

★★★★ **The Seven Year Itch** 1955   105 mins (cert 12)
Tom Ewell is the middle-aged man attracted, during his wife's
absence, to the blonde upstairs, *Marilyn Monroe*. Lovely Billy
Wilder comedy, notable for the famous skirt-lifting scene.

★★ **Shadows and Fog** 1992   89 mins (cert 15)
Black-and-white pre-war Europe examined by *Woody Allen*. *Mia
Farrow*, *Madonna*, *John Malkovich*, *Jodie Foster*, etc, appear. Not
one of Allen's best.

★★ **Shag** 1988   98 mins (cert 15)
Four high school students head for the beach for a shag. No, not
that – this shag is a dance. *Phoebe Cates*, *Scott Caffrey* and *Bridget
Fonda* head a likeable cast.

★★★ **She's Gotta Have It** 1986   84 mins (cert 18)
Spike Lee's highly promising first feature examines the pros and
cons of being a liberated modern woman. *Tracy Camilla Johns* is
the girl choosing between three lovers.

★★ **She's Having a Baby** 1988   106 mins (cert 15)
A bland John Hughes comedy with *Kevin Bacon* as the newly-wed
having second thoughts about marriage to *Elizabeth McGovern*
and his impending fatherhood.

★★ **Sibling Rivalry** 1990   88 mins (cert 15)
Nice comic idea, shame about the script. Repressed housewife,
Kirstie Alley, has brief affair with stranger who not only dies but
turns out to be her husband's long lost brother.

★★★ **Sister Act** 1992   100 mins (cert PG)
Whoopi Goldberg plays a nightclub singer hiding from the Mob in
a convent – like hiding a raven in a dovecote. Mother superior
Maggie Smith lets her join the choir with delightful results.

★★★★★ **Sleeper** 1973   88 mins (cert 15)
Lovely stuff from *Woody Allen* as a man deep-frozen for 200 years who awakes in a world where alcohol and smoking are good for you.

★★★★ **Sleepless in Seattle** 1993   95 mins (cert PG)
Feel-good romantic comedy in which *Meg Ryan* hears widower *Tom Hanks* talking on the radio and falls in love. Charming.

★★★★ **The Snapper** 1992   91 mins (cert 15)
A delightful Roddy Doyle story about the effects of unmarried pregnancy on an Irish family. Delightful cast well-directed by Stephen Frears.

★★★ **Soapdish** 1991   96 mins (cert 12)
Offbeat comedy following the off-camera lives of a soap opera cast, including *Sally Field* and *Kevin Kline*.

★★★ **Soft Top, Hard Shoulder** 1993   95 mins (cert 15)
Gently engaging comedy about *Peter Capaldi*'s accident-prone attempt to get himself to Glasgow in time for his father's 60th birthday.

★★★ **So I Married an Axe Murderer** 1993   95 mins (cert 12)
Mike Myers suspects the woman of his dreams is a notorious axe murderer. Patchy comedy much helped by amusing cameos from *Alan Arkin* and *Charles Grodin*.

★★★★★ **Some Like It Hot** 1959   122 mins (cert U)
Billy Wilder's classic comedy. *Jack Lemmon* and *Tony Curtis* pose as members of *Marilyn Monroe*'s all-female band to escape gangsters.

★★★★ **Splash** 1984   110 mins (cert PG)
Deliciously funny fairytale set in modern-day New York where *Tom Hanks* unwittingly falls in love with a mermaid, *Darryl Hannah*.

★★ **Splitting Heirs** 1992   86 mins (cert 12)
Largely disappointing comedy of mistaken identity and lost inheritances by and starring *Eric Idle* with *Rick Moranis*, *Barbara Hershey* and *Catherine Zeta Jones*.

★★ **Stop! or My Mom Will Shoot** 1992   87 mins (cert PG)
Comedy's not *Sylvester Stallone*'s strong point but as a cop backed up by his feisty mother, *Estelle Getty*, he has a certain charm.

★★★ **Straight Talk** 1992   91 mins (cert PG)
Small-town girl *Dolly Parton* lands a job as radio agony aunt in
Chicago. Investigating journalist *James Woods* is intrigued.
Delightful romantic comedy/drama.

★★★ **Strictly Ballroom** 1992   91 mins (cert PG)
Surprisingly enjoyable romantic comedy set in the competitive
world of Australian ballroom dancing. Fast, cheerful, funny film.

★★★ **Suburban Commando** 1991   90 mins (cert PG)
Wrestler *Hulk Hogan* stars as a fighter from another planet in a
riotous farce which is much funnier and more satisfying than
you'd expect.

★★★★ **The Sunshine Boys** 1975   111 mins (cert U)
Hilarious Neil Simon comedy of an ageing, sparring showbiz
duo, *Walter Matthau* and *George Burns*, reunited reluctantly for a
big TV show.

★★★ **The Supergrass** 1985   105 mins (cert 15)
Amusing tale of smuggling at the seaside from the Comic Strip
team with all the regulars – *Robbie Coltrane*, *Ade Edmondson* and
Alexei Sayle among others.

★★★ **The Sure Thing** 1985   94 mins (cert 15)
Rob Reiner's deft direction of *John Cusack* and *Daphne Zuniga* as
two young college students sharing an amusing, adventure-
strewn, love-torn ride home.

★★ **Switch** 1992   103 mins (cert 15)
Murdered chauvinist returns with a man's mind but *Ellen
Barkin*'s body. An uneasy comedy, light on laughs.

★★ **Switching Channels** 1988   105 mins (cert PG)
'The Front Page' now set in a modern TV news station. *Burt
Reynolds*, *Kathleen Turner* and *Christopher Reeve* can't quite make it
work.

★★★★ **The Talk of the Town** 1942   118 mins (cert U)
Great romantic comedy. *Cary Grant* as an escaped convict hiding
out in *Jean Arthur*'s home, rented by Supreme Court judge
Ronald Colman.

★★ **The Tall Guy** 1989   92 mins (cert 15)
Jeff Goldblum plays the fall-guy to *Rowan Atkinson*'s comic until he
meets nurse, *Emma Thompson*. Pleasing movie; not as good as it
should have been.

★★★★ **The Taming of the Shrew** 1967   122 mins (cert U)
Franco Zeffirelli's zesty, colourful version of Shakespeare's sex-
war comedy featuring *Elizabeth Taylor* and *Richard Burton*.

★★★ **Tango** 1993   88 mins (cert 15)
Comedy from 'Hairdresser's Husband' director Patrice Leconte.
Womanizing husband tries to murder his unfaithful wife who's
had enough of his infidelity.

★★★ **'10'** 1979   122 mins (cert 18)
Male menopause hits *Dudley Moore* in a pretty good comedy co-
starring a disrobed *Bo Derek* (whose looks score a perfect ten)
and *Julie Andrews*.

★★★ **That Sinking Feeling** 1979   93 mins (cert 15)
Rollicking Bill Forsyth film about a group of young unemployed
Glaswegians turning to crime unsuccessfully.

★★★ **Things Change** 1988   100 mins (cert PG)
Shoemaker *Don Ameche* agrees to take the rap for a Mafia killer.
As a reward, *Joe Mantegna* takes him on a lavish fling before he
gives himself up. Moving and funny.

★★ **This Is My Life** 1992   94 mins (cert 12)
Nora Ephron's tale of two sisters growing up in the shadow of
their show-biz mother, *Julie Kavner*. Amiable but uneventful.

★★★★ **This Is Spinal Tap** 1984   82 mins (cert 15)
Wicked parody of rock bands and music documentaries.
Narrated and directed by *Rob Reiner*.

★★★ **Three Men and a Baby** 1987   102 mins (cert PG)
Lively comedy about three confirmed bachelors – *Ted Danson*,
Tom Selleck and *Steve Guttenberg* – whose lives are disrupted when
a baby girl is left on their doorstep.

★ **Three Men and a Little Lady** 1990   104 mins (cert PG)
Crass sequel sees the boys trying to stop young Mary being
taken to England by her mother, *Nancy Travis*.

★★★ **Three of Hearts** 1993   105 mins (cert 18)
Offbeat and quite funny romantic comedy in which two lesbians
– *Kelly Lynch* and *Sherilyn Fenn* – use and abuse male escort
William Baldwin.

★★ **Throw Momma from the Train** 1987   88 mins (cert 15)
Thin comedy in which *Danny DeVito* and *Billy Crystal* exchange
murders. (Hitchcock did it straight and much better with
'Strangers on a Train'.)

★★★★ **The Time Bandits** 1981   116 mins (cert 15)
Ralph Richardson and six dwarfs escort a young boy through time
in a hilarious romp amply spiced with guest stars. *Ian Holm*
marvellous as tiny Napoleon.

★★★ **Tin Men** 1987   112 mins (cert 15)
Danny DeVito and *Richard Dreyfuss* paired as loser and hustler,
brought together by a car crash in a warmly amusing tale.

★★★★ **The Titfield Thunderbolt** 1953   84 mins (cert U)
Unadulterated fun from Ealing. Group of villagers, led by *Stanley
Holloway* and *Sid James*, fighting to keep their beloved railway.

★★★★★ **To Be or Not To Be** 1942   99 mins (cert PG)
Jack Benny and *Carole Lombard* lead this delightful Ernst Lubitsch
farce of a group of actors posing as Nazis in war-torn Poland.
Glorious bad taste.

★★ **To Be or Not To Be** 1983   107 mins (cert PG)
A quite unnecessary remake; much cruder, much less funny.
The stars this time are *Mel Brooks* and *Anne Bancroft*.

★★ **Tom and Jerry: The Movie** 1993   83 mins (cert U)
Spoilt by talking and singing. Tom and Jerry's real fans will
stick to the shorts.

★★★★ **Tom Jones** 1963   128 mins (cert PG)
Sprightly version of Henry Fielding's 18th-century novel about a
young man's bawdy experiences. *Albert Finney* excellent in title
role.

★★ **Too Hot to Handle** 1991   117 mins (cert 15)
Alec Baldwin and *Kim Basinger* as the star-crossed lovers in this
romantic comedy set in 1950s. The couple fell in love and
subsequently married in real life – ahhh.

★★★★ **Tootsie** 1982   116 mins (cert PG)
Outstanding performance by *Dustin Hoffman* as an actor who
passes himself off as a woman in order to get work. Sparkling
comedy.

★★ **Top Secret!** 1984   90 mins (cert 15)
Not bad spy spoof from the 'Airplane!' team. *Val Kilmer* is the
pop star accidentally involved with Nazis and the like on a tour
of Eastern Europe.

★★ **Toys** 1993   121 mins (cert PG)
Robin Williams as eccentric heir to toy factory threatened by
uncle, *Michael Gambon*, who wants to turn it into a weapons
factory. Visually outstanding but weak and disjointed story.

★★★ **Trading Places** 1988   119 mins (cert 15)
Down-and-out, *Eddie Murphy*, and spoilt rich kid, *Dan Aykroyd*,
manipulated into swapping lives. Great fun, marred by soppy
climax on train.

★★ **True Identity** 1991   95 mins (cert 15)
Lenny Henry as an actor hunted by the Mob disguises himself as,
among other things, a white man. Great make-up but Henry
much better than the script.

★★ **Twins** 1988   112 mins (cert PG)
Reasonably comic adventures ensue when unlikely twins, *Danny
DeVito* and *Arnold Schwarzenegger* – separated at birth – are
reunited.

★ **Uncle Buck** 1989   100 mins (cert 12)
John Candy, the slobbish relative of the title, babysitting his
brother's brattish kids. Feeble comedy of little substance.

★★ **Used People** 1992   115 mins (cert 15)
Romantic Jewish comedy wherein Jewish widow *Shirley MacLaine*
finds love the second time around with an Italian, *Marcello
Mastroianni*.

★★ **Vampire's Kiss** 1989   103 mins (cert 18)
Horror spoof which falls apart as literary agent, *Nicolas Cage*,
imagines he's a vampire after lusty *Jennifer Beals* bites him.

★★ **Vice Versa** 1988   98 mins (cert PG)
Judge Reinhold and son, *Fred Savage*, swap bodies in thin, but well-
played, role-reversal comedy.

★★★ **WarGames** 1983   113 mins (cert PG)
Computer whizzkid, *Matthew Broderick*, creates enjoyable havoc
when he taps into American defence programme.

★★★★ **The War of the Roses** 1989 111 mins (cert 15)
Achingly funny black comedy about marriage turning sour.
Kathleen Turner and *Michael Douglas* as warring partners. No one
contemplating marriage – or divorce – should miss it.

★★ **Wayne's World** 1992 95 mins (cert PG)
A lesser, more streetwise 'Bill and Ted'. *Mike Myers* and *Dana
Carvey*, hosts of a cult TV show broadcast from a basement, are
exploited by *Rob Lowe*. The occasional flash of comedy.

★★★ **Wayne's World 2** 1994 100 mins (cert PG)
A rare occasion of the sequel being better than the original.
Here dastardly *Christopher Walken* has designs on Wayne's
girlfriend, *Tia Carrere*.

★ **Weekend at Bernie's** 1989 99 mins (cert 12)
Two lads in fairly amusing trouble when trying to pretend their
dead host is still alive and well.

★★★ **Welcome Home, Roxy Carmichael** 1990 95 mins (cert 12)
Enigmatic comedy about a lonely young girl, *Winona Ryder*,
adapting to adoption and relationships.

★ **We're No Angels** 1989 106 mins (cert 15)
Robert De Niro and *Sean Penn* look uncomfortable as escaped
convicts passing as priests in a feeble comic remake.

★★★ **What About Bob?** 1991 110 mins (cert PG)
Psychiatrist *Richard Dreyfuss* is driven mad when his neurotic
patient, *Bill Murray*, follows him on a family holiday. Very funny.

★★★★ **Whatever Happened to Baby Jane?** 1962 132 mins (cert 18)
Wild, over-the-top black comedy of two sisters tormenting one
another. Magnificently hammy performances by a demented
Bette Davis and a crippled *Joan Crawford*.

★★★★ **What's Up Doc?** 1972 94 mins (cert U)
Great comedy of errors based on a mix-up of mismatched
couples. *Ryan O'Neal* and *Barbra Streisand* lead.

★★★★ **When Harry Met Sally** 1989 95 mins (cert 15)
Billy Crystal and *Meg Ryan* put paid to the theory that men and
women can have a platonic relationship in delightful tale,
featuring THAT fake orgasm scene.

★★★★★ **Whisky Galore** 1949   82 mins (cert U)
Rich, classic Ealing comedy about a small Scottish community
stealing cache of whisky from wartime shipwreck.

★★★ **White Men Can't Jump** 1992   112 mins (cert 15)
Wesley Snipes and *Woody Harrelson* as a pair of basketball hustlers
in a nicely offbeat comedy. (In Europe the film was called
'White Men Can't Get It Up'.)

★ **Wild West** 1993   85 mins (cert 15)
Ragged comedy/drama about young Asians in South London
trying to break away from poverty trap through music.

★★ **Wilt** 1988   91 mins (cert 15)
A blow-up doll causes comic problems for detective *Mel Smith*
and murder suspect, *Griff Rhys-Jones*.

★★★ **Wish You Were Here** 1987   92 mins (cert 15)
Bittersweet seaside comedy about a young girl's sexual growing-
up in wartime Britain. Remarkable performance by young *Emily
Lloyd*.

★★★ **The Witches of Eastwick** 1987   118 mins (cert 18)
Three beautiful women – *Cher*, *Susan Sarandon* and *Michelle
Pfeiffer* – seduced by the devilish *Jack Nicholson*. Good fun.

★★ **Withnail & I** 1987   105 mins (cert 15)
1960s-based British comedy. Unemployed actors, *Richard E
Grant* and *Paul McGann*, leave life of drink and drugs in London
for disastrous country holiday.

★★★ **Working Girl** 1988   113 mins (cert 15)
Sophisticated comedy of errors. *Melanie Griffith* is an upwardly-
mobile secretary, *Sigourney Weaver* her ruthless boss. *Harrison
Ford* provides the love interest.

★★★ **Young Frankenstein** 1974   106 mins (cert 15)
Funny, farcical parody of Hollywood horror movies by Mel
Brooks. *Gene Wilder* as the mad scientist, *Madeline Kahn* his
fiancée who becomes the monster's wife.

★★★ **Zelig** 1983   79 mins (cert PG)
Woody Allen as ubiquitous human chameleon who hob-nobs with
Hitler and others. Great editing and marvellous trick
photography.

DRAMA

★★★ **Accident** 1967   105 mins (cert PG)
Dirk Bogarde as Oxford tutor in study of events leading to death
of a girl student. Sharp, cerebral script by Harold Pinter. Joseph
Losey directed.

★★ **Accidental Hero** 1992   116 mins (cert 15)
Dustin Hoffman saves plane crash survivors but hobo *Andy Garcia*
claims the reward – and the admiration of TV journalist *Geena
Davis*.

★★ **Accidental Tourist** 1988   121 mins (cert PG)
William Hurt as a travel writer whose emotional journey through
divorce makes for bleak drama lightened by *Geena Davis'*
comic touch.

★★★★ **The Accused** 1988   110 mins (cert 18)
Brilliantly executed rape drama. Victim, Oscar-winner *Jodie
Foster*, and lawyer, *Kelly McGillis*, fight for justice.

★★ **After Darkness** 1985   109 mins (cert 15)
Dangerous study of schizophrenia in which a man tries to cure
his brother with perilous results. *John Hurt* and *Julian Sands* star.

★★★★ **The Age of Innocence** 1993   125 mins (cert 15)
Lavish period drama from Martin Scorsese set in New York in
19th century. *Daniel Day-Lewis* as the Victorian fiancé of *Winona
Ryder* but hopelessly in love with widowed *Michelle Pfeiffer*.

★★★ **Agnes of God** 1985   98 mins (cert 15)
Psychiatrist, *Jane Fonda*, is called to convent where a nun is
suspected of murdering her baby. Poignant drama.

★★★ **Alice Doesn't Live Here Any More** 1975   108 mins (cert 15)
Ellen Burstyn as the widow coming to terms with her own life
after the death of her husband in Martin Scorsese's tender,
thoughtful movie.

★★★★★ **All About Eve** 1950   138 mins (cert U)
A volatile actress, *Bette Davis*, fastens her seatbelt for a bumpy
ride when she befriends *Anne Baxter*'s insinuating Eve. Brilliant
drama of the old school.

★★★★ All the President's Men 1976   138 mins (cert 15)
Compelling account of how Washington Post journalists, *Dustin Hoffman* and *Robert Redford*, exposed the Watergate scandal. Gripping stuff.

★★★ All This and Heaven Too 1940   143 mins (cert U)
Ill-fated romance between French nobleman, *Charles Boyer*, and governess, *Bette Davis*. Weepy melodrama.

★★★ Always 1985   123 mins (cert PG)
Spielberg's charming romance of the old school sees *Richard Dreyfuss* as ghostly guardian angel to old flame *Holly Hunter*.

★★★★ Amadeus 1984   158 mins (cert PG)
Oscar-winning examination of rivalry between envious court composer Salieri, *F Murray Abraham*, and scatological young upstart Mozart, *Tom Hulce*.

★★ American Heart 1993   114 mins (cert 15)
Paroled convict, *Jeff Bridges*, and teenage son, *Edward Furlong*, fight the odds in a doomed search for a better future. Well-played but bleak drama.

★★ Amongst Friends 1993   88 mins (cert 18)
Follows the transition of three privileged boys into manhood as they muscle into racketeering – tears before bedtime guaranteed.

★★ And Justice For All 1979   119 mins (cert PG)
Behind the scenes shenanigans of the Maryland justice system is a confused show-case for *Al Pacino*'s talents.

★★★ Another Country 1984   90 mins (cert 15)
Beautiful and touching story about a future spy's boyhood. (Guy Burgess was the inspiration.) *Rupert Everett* and *Colin Firth* excel as the rebellious public school boys.

★★★ Another Time, Another Place 1983   102 mins (cert PG)
Phyllis Logan as the Scottish farmer's wife who falls in love with an Italian POW in WWII. Very nicely done.

★★ Assassin of the Tsar 1991   104 mins (cert 12)
Good performance by *Malcolm McDowell* as a schizophrenic who claims he murdered the Russian Tsar in 1881. Rather unconvincing script, though.

★★★ **Atlantic City** 1981   105 mins (cert 15)
Louis Malle's wickedly observant character study of winners and losers in America's famous gambling resort. Probably *Burt Lancaster*'s best performance.

★★ **Aunt Julia and the Scriptwriter** 1991   107 mins (cert 12)
Budding radio writer *Keanu Reeves* falls for his aunt, *Barbara Hershey*, in 1950s New Orleans. *Peter Falk* takes the acting honours in a film that should have been better.

★ **Avalon** 1990   128 mins (cert U)
Despite a strong cast, Barry Levinson's vaguely autobiographical story of a family of Russian Jewish immigrants to America fails to grip.

★★★★ **Awakenings** 1990   121 mins (cert 12)
Outstanding performances mark this traumatic true tale of a doctor, *Robin Williams*, helping encephalitic patients – notably *Robert De Niro* as his guinea pig.

★ **The Baby of Macon** 1993   120 mins (cert 18)
Peter Greenaway abandons the thin storyline of a Christ-like child in favour of imagery. Visually spectacular but self-indulgent and deeply pretentious.

★★★ **The Bad and the Beautiful** 1952   118 mins (cert PG)
Great performances by *Kirk Douglas* as ruthless Hollywood producer and *Lana Turner* as a victimized star.

★★★ **Badlands** 1973   94 mins (cert 18)
Disturbing account of notorious Starkweather–Fugate spate of killings in 1950s – led by *Martin Sheen* and *Sissy Spacek*. Terrence Malick's first and best film, which now enjoys a cult following.

★★★ **Bad Lieutenant** 1992   96 mins (cert 18)
Due to violent subject matter this film had difficulty getting a BBFC certificate for video. Disturbing rape of nun and unpleasant resolution just some of the problems facing burnt-out detective *Harvey Keitel*, who gives superb performance.

★★ **Bad Timing** 1980   123 mins (cert 18)
Nicolas Roeg's eclectic psychodrama of a Vienna-based affair between attempted suicide, *Theresa Russell*, and her psychoanalyst, *Art Garfunkel*.

★★★ **Barry Lyndon** 1975   187 mins (cert PG)
Breathtaking photography in Stanley Kubrick's lengthy, variable
version of Thackerey's story about the adventures of an 18th-
century Irish rogue. *Ryan O'Neal* not quite up to the title role.

....

★ **Beaches** 1988   124 mins (cert 15)
Unashamedly over-sentimental tale of love and loss between
childhood friends *Bette Midler* and *Barbara Hershey*.

....

★★★ **The Belly of an Architect** 1987   118 mins (cert 15)
Peter Greenaway's great to look at but enigmatic tale of a dying
architect, *Brian Dennehy*, in Rome. Dennehy lends impressive
human warmth to a cool story.

....

★★★ **Benny and Joon** 1993   95 mins (cert PG)
Aidan Quinn looks after daffy sister *Mary Stuart Masterson* until
Johnny Depp moves in. Marching to a different drummer, he and
Masterson fall in love. Whimsical drama with touch of magic in
more ways than one.

....

★ **The Big Blue** 1988   119 mins (cert 15)
Water-logged tale of insurance investigator, *Rosanna Arquette*,
trailing her boyfriend around diving competitions. Luc Besson
directed but why did he bother?

....

★★★★ **The Big Chill** 1983   103 mins (cert 15)
Intelligent direction by Lawrence Kasdan of an absorbing story
of college friends reuniting in mid-life. With *Tom Berenger*, *Glenn
Close*, *Jeff Goldblum* and *William Hurt*. *Kevin Costner* was in it, too,
but his entire role ended on the cutting-room floor.

....

★★ **Billy Bathgate** 1991   107 mins (cert 15)
Young lad yearns to join ranks of *Dustin Hoffman*'s mob in 1930s
overlong gangster story. *Bruce Willis* and *Nicole Kidman* co-star.
Hoffman not menacing enough as Dutch Schulz.

....

★★★ **Billy Liar** 1963   98 mins (cert PG)
Tom Courtenay plays a day dreamer escaping from dreary life in a
smashing adaptation of Keith Waterhouse's novel of Walter
Mittyism and gritty north country drama.

....

★★★ **Birdy** 1984   120 mins (cert 15)
Vietnam-traumatized *Matthew Modine* yearns to fly. *Nicolas Cage*
is the friend determined to help him in Alan Parker's
thoughtful study of the effects of war.

★★★★ Black Narcissus 1946   98 mins (cert PG)
Deborah Kerr and young *Jean Simmons* in Powell/Pressburger story of the emotional and sexual problems facing a group of nuns in the Himalayas.

....

★★ Blaze 1989   129 mins (cert 18)
Promising but disappointing account of Louisiana governor Earl Long's fateful affair with a stripper, *Lolita Davidovich*. Based on real life. *Paul Newman* fine as the governor.

....

★ Blindside 1987   98 mins (cert 18)
Harvey Keitel as the surveillance expert inadvertently drawn into gang rivalry. All rather confused and messy.

....

★★ Blood In, Blood Out 1993   181 mins (cert 18)
Three Hispanics in Los Angeles follow vastly different paths in life – a cop, a convict, a drug-addicted painter. Violent, uninvolving and far too long.

....

★★★ Bodies Rest and Motion 1993   96 mins (cert 15)
Offbeat tale of romance and relationships with interesting, attractive young cast – *Bridget Fonda*, *Tim Roth*, *Eric Stoltz*, *Phoebe Cates*. Fonda shines as the one who eventually finds freedom.

....

★★★ The Bodyguard 1992   130 mins (cert 15)
Diva *Whitney Houston*, pestered by death threats, further complicates her life by employing an attractive bodyguard, *Kevin Costner*. Romantic goings-on are thus inevitable. Undemanding and enjoyable. (Houston provides the pleasing soundtrack.)

....

★★★ Born on the Fourth of July 1989   151 mins (cert 18)
Tom Cruise superb as embittered, crippled army veteran in Oliver Stone's Oscar-winning Vietnam movie, part two of his war trilogy that began with 'Platoon'.

....

★ Boxing Helena 1993   107 mins (cert 18)
Unintentionally funny story of obsessed doctor *Julian Sands* imprisoning the object of his desire, *Sherilyn Fenn*, by removing her arms and legs. It cost Kim Basinger $6 million when she walked away from this turkey. Money well spent.

....

★★★ Boyz N the Hood 1991   111 mins (cert 15)
Black teenagers struggle to survive in drug-ridden South Central LA. Bleak but leaving room for hope. Notable debut by director John Singleton.

★★★ **Breakfast at Tiffany's** 1961   115 mins (cert PG)
Touching love story involving cute call-girl, *Audrey Hepburn*, and writer *George Peppard*. Good score.

....

★★★ **The Breakfast Club** 1984   93 mins (cert 15)
John Hughes' comic teen flick set in school detention class. Brat Pack cast headed by *Emilio Estevez* and *Molly Ringwald*.

....

★★★ **Brian's Song** 1970   73 mins (cert PG)
Warming, true-life tale of friendship in face of adversity and rivalry between American footballers *James Caan* and *Billy Dee Williams*.

....

★★★★ **Brideshead Revisited** 1981   664 mins (cert 15)
The award-winning ITV series now available on video and a must for any household.

....

★★★ **Brief Encounter** 1945   86 mins (cert PG)
Dated but still charming David Lean classic telling of doomed love affair between *Trevor Howard* and *Celia Johnson*.

....

★★ **Bright Lights, Big City** 1988   104 mins (cert 18)
Michael J Fox as the kid who comes to New York to find success and is caught up in a life of drugs, sex and alcohol.

....

★★★ **A Bronx Tale** 1994   120 mins (cert 18)
Robert De Niro's accomplished debut as a director with a gently absorbing tale of a young Bronx boy's friendship with the local Mafia honcho.

....

★★★ **Bugsy** 1991   135 mins (cert 18)
Warren Beatty plays the hood who 'invented' Las Vegas as a gambling resort. Overlong but good performances.

....

★★★ **Bull Durham** 1988   108 mins (cert 15)
Kevin Costner and *Susan Sarandon* try to nurture the talents of promising baseballer *Tim Robbins*. Neat, underrated story.

....

★★★ **Bus Stop** 1956   96 mins (cert U)
Comedy/drama of a rodeo star, *Don Murray*, pursuing sexy showgirl, *Marilyn Monroe*, in one of her best roles.

....

★★★ **Buster** 1988   103 mins (cert 15)
Phil Collins more than adequately portrays the Great Train Robber but *Julie Walters* shines as Mr Edwards' wife.

★★ **The Butcher's Wife** 1991   105 mins (cert 12)
Sporadic laughs in romantic story about a clairvoyant, *Demi Moore*, who moves in and changes the neighbourhood.

★★★ **The Caine Mutiny** 1954   125 mins (cert U)
Two naval officers court-martialled for mutiny against paranoid captain. *Humphrey Bogart* leads excellent cast.

★★★ **Cal** 1984   102 mins (cert 15)
Exceptional drama of an Irish teenager, *John Lynch*, trying to sever ties with IRA and falling for *Helen Mirren*.

★★★ **The Candidate** 1972   110 mins (cert PG)
Sharply cynical look at American politics. *Robert Redford* runs for the Senate on integrity ticket only because he thinks he can't win.

★★★ **Carnal Knowledge** 1971   97 mins (cert 18)
Jack Nicholson and *Art Garfunkel* change attitudes and sexual hang-ups as they mature from college optimism to middle-aged angst. Mike Nichols directed.

★★★ **Carve Her Name with Pride** 1958   119 mins (cert U)
Moving WWII biopic of young British widow, *Virginia McKenna*, enlisted as spy to help French resistance. Marvellous tale of heroism.

★★★★ **Casablanca** 1942   102 mins (cert U)
Quite simply one of the great movie romances, set in Morocco with *Humphrey Bogart* and *Ingrid Bergman*, not to mention *Claude Rains*.

★★ **Catch 22** 1970   122 mins (cert 15)
Alan Arkin leads good cast in Mike Nichols' disappointing attempt to bring Joseph Heller's brilliant anti-war novel to the screen.

★★★ **Cat on a Hot Tin Roof** 1958   108 mins (cert 15)
Sparring couple, *Elizabeth Taylor* and *Paul Newman*, in goodish adaptation of Tennessee Williams' scorching melodrama. *Burl Ives* great as Big Daddy.

★★ **Cat on a Hot Tin Roof** 1976   100 mins (cert 15)
Fairish TV adaptation of the above. *Laurence Olivier* fine in Burl Ives role; *Natalie Wood* OK as Taylor-substitute.

★★ The Cement Garden 1993   105 mins (cert 18)
Ian McEwan's downbeat tale of incest between strange siblings
after their parents die. Rather glum vehicle for *Sinead Cusack*
and *Charlotte Gainsborough*.

★★ The Cemetery Club 1993   102 mins (cert 12)
Three widows searching for love again. *Olympia Dukakis*, *Ellen
Burstyn* and *Diane Ladd* all rather better than the story.

★★★ Chaplin 1992   144 mins (cert 12)
Richard Attenborough's solid biopic of the little comic greatly
enhanced by the title performance from *Robert Downey Jr*. Fine
support from *Anthony Hopkins*, *James Woods*, *Dan Aykroyd* and
Kevin Kline.

★★★★ Chariots of Fire 1981   121 mins (cert U)
Oscar-winning and absorbing story of two British sprinters and
their successful bid for gold medals in 1924 Olympics.

★★ Children of a Lesser God 1986   119 mins (cert 15)
Touching love affair between a teacher, *William Hurt*, and his
deaf student, *Marlee Matlin*.

★★★★★ Citizen Kane 1941   119 mins (cert U)
One of the best films ever made. *Orson Welles* was a mere 24
when he directed and starred in it. Everyone should see it.

★★ City of Joy 1991   135 mins (cert 12)
Calcutta slums form backdrop of intelligent but over-earnest
drama with *Patrick Swayze* and *Pauline Collins*. A good try.

★★ Clean and Sober 1988   124 mins (cert 18)
Tough examination of drug and booze addiction enhanced by
Michael Keaton's performance.

★★ Close My Eyes 1991   107 mins (cert 18)
Sibling incest forms basis of unusual English drama lightened
by presence of *Alan Rickman*.

★★ Cocktail 1988   104 mins (cert 15)
Tom Cruise tends bar, services women and juggles a very good
cocktail too in a pretty pointless romantic drama.

★★ **The Color of Money** 1986   119 mins (cert 15)
So-so sequel to 'The Hustler' pairs sex symbols *Tom Cruise* and *Paul Newman* in battle of green baize. Oscar for Newman.

★★ **The Color Purple** 1985   152 mins (cert 15)
Spielberg's over-lavish, unconvincing story of a young black woman's hard life and times in American south. *Whoopi Goldberg* stars.

★★★ **Colors** 1988   116 mins (cert 18)
An ageing cop, *Robert Duvall*, and his young partner, *Sean Penn*, take on the urban gangs of LA in a meandering story that works rather well.

★★ **Come See the Paradise** 1990   131 mins (cert 15)
Alan Parker's worthy exposé of the persecution of Japanese Americans in USA during WWII. *Dennis Quaid* leads but can't lighten the all-too-heavy tone.

★★ **The Company of Wolves** 1984   95 mins (cert 15)
Freudian but unsatisfying adult version of Little Red Riding Hood. Good sets and costumes.

★★ **The Connection** 1961   110 mins (cert 18)
Tough drama of documentary director filming a group of junkies awaiting their next fix.

★★★★ **The Cook, the Thief, His Wife and Her Lover** 1989   120 mins (cert 18)
Peter Greenaway's visually astonishing black comedy set in restaurant owned by greedy gang boss, *Michael Gambon*. Horrifying as well as funny.

★★★★ **Cool Hand Luke** 1967   126 mins (cert 15)
Convict *Paul Newman* as individual fighting penal system. Similar in theme (and compares favourably) to 'One Flew Over the Cuckoo's Nest'.

★★★ **The Cotton Club** 1984   128 mins (cert 15)
Francis Coppola's flawed but vivid drama centred on famous Harlem nightclub and rise of the Mafia.

★★ **Coupe de Ville** 1990   98 mins (cert 12)
Three squabbling brothers ordered by dominant father to drive Cadillac across USA. Weak comedy, heavy sentimentality, but *Alan Arkin* is excellent.

★★★ **Cry Freedom** 1987   158 mins (cert PG)
Richard Attenborough's fiercely anti-apartheid drama tells of
the friendship between South African journalist Donald Woods,
Kevin Kline, and black activist Steve Biko, *Denzel Washington*.

★★★ **The Crying Game** 1992   112 mins (cert 18)
IRA hitman, *Stephen Rea*, escapes the cause by going to London
where he meets mysterious *Jaye Davidson* – more twists than a
corkscrew will keep you guessing from start to finish.
Fascinating stuff.

★★★ **A Cry in the Dark** 1988   121 mins (cert 15)
Based on the 'Dingo Baby' case in Australia. *Meryl Streep* is
exceptional as mother wrongly accused of infanticide.

★ **The Cutting Edge** 1992   102 mins (cert PG)
Dumb, sentimental tale of ice-hockey star and his romance with
a Russian figure-skater. *D B Sweeney* and *Moira Kelly* are OK
though.

★ **Dad** 1989   118 mins (cert PG)
Slushy father and son reconciliation drama with *Jack Lemmon*
seriously miscast as irascible father to *Ted Danson*.

★★★ **Dance with a Stranger** 1985   102 mins (cert 15)
Fine British reconstruction of events leading to hanging of Ruth
Ellis. Brilliant portrayal of murderess by *Miranda Richardson*.
Rupert Everett is her lover.

★★★★ **Dangerous Liaisons** 1988   120 mins (cert 15)
Sexual games and corruption in 18th-century France, starring
Glenn Close, *John Malkovich* and *Michelle Pfeiffer* in excellent
Stephen Frears film.

★★★ **Dark Victory** 1939   106 mins (cert PG)
Dying *Bette Davis* falls in love with doctor in weepy melodrama.
Davis on top form, *Humphrey Bogart* woefully miscast.

★★★ **Darling** 1965   122 mins (cert 15)
Very stylish, very Sixties story of a young fashion model, Oscar-
winning *Julie Christie*, and the men – *Dirk Bogarde*, *Laurence
Harvey* – she uses to help her climb the social ladder.

★ **Daughters of the Dust** 1993   113 mins (cert PG)
Set amongst the Gullah people in the early 1900s who lived off
the coast of Georgia. An African American family headed by
88-year-old matriarch gathers for their last evening before they
leave the island for the mainland.

★★★ **The Day of the Jackal** 1973   142 mins (cert 15)
Suspenseful but inevitably predictable political drama sees
Edward Fox as assassin gunning for French president Charles de
Gaulle.

★★★ **Days of Heaven** 1978   95 mins (cert PG)
Ménage-à-trois among the mid-west wheatfields in 1916. With
Richard Gere, *Brooke Adams* and *Sam Shepard*. Box office flop at the
time but brilliantly directed by Terrence Malik.

★★★★ **The Dead** 1987   83 mins (cert U)
Superb adaptation by John Huston (his last film) of James Joyce
story. *Anjelica Huston* heads a terrific – and otherwise Irish –
cast.

★★★★ **Dead Poets Society** 1989   129 mins (cert PG)
Peter Weir's moving, thoughtful drama of unorthodox teacher
Robin Williams and his effect, for good and ill, on his pupils.

★★★ **Death in Venice** 1971   128 mins (cert 15)
Visconti's slow, beautiful version of Thomas Mann novel with
Dirk Bogarde as dying artist obsessed with young boy.

★★★★ **The Deer Hunter** 1978   183 mins (cert 18)
Powerful, painful, Oscar-winning story of young Pittsburgh
workers before, during and after Vietnam war. *Robert De Niro*
and *Meryl Streep* head a strong cast.

★ **Desperate Remedies** 1993   93 mins (cert 12)
Bizarre New Zealand melodrama – a sort of opera without the
arias – about convoluted 19th-century sex, politics and big
business. Nice, but not altogether successful attempt at
something different.

★★★ **Diner** 1982   110 mins (cert 15)
Thoughtful, funny, inconsequential tale of a group of friends
(including *Ellen Barkin* and *Mickey Rourke*) hanging out in a
Baltimore cafe in the late 1950s.

★ **Dinner at Eight** 1989   92 mins (cert 15)
Shabby TV remake of fine 1930s movie. Events leading up to elegant dinner party. *Lauren Bacall* heads excellent cast.

- -

★ **Dirty Weekend** 1993   102 mins (cert 18)
Lia Williams takes revenge on men after Peeping Tom pushes her too far. Distasteful, exploitative movie bearing the most crass hallmarks of its director, Michael Winner.

- -

★★★ **Distant Voices, Still Lives** 1988   85 mins (cert 15)
Haunting, stylized memories of a working-class family and its births, deaths and marriages in post-war England.

- -

★★★ **The Doctor** 1992   123 mins (cert 12)
Surgeon, *William Hurt*, reviews flippant attitude to medical profession when he finds himself on other end of scalpel. *Elizabeth McGovern* as fellow cancer sufferer.

- -

★★★★ **Doctor Zhivago** 1965   192 mins (cert 15)
David Lean's lush treatment of *Julie Christie* and *Omar Shariff*'s ill-starred romance during Russian Revolution.

- -

★★★★ **Dog Day Afternoon** 1975   130 mins (cert 15)
Al Pacino terrific as loser who robs bank so lover can have sex-change op. The raid – but not the film – goes disastrously wrong.

- -

★★ **The Doors** 1991   141 mins (cert 18)
Oliver Stone's interesting, but overlong version of the life of Jim Morrison, *Val Kilmer*, and those around him, including *Meg Ryan*.

- -

★★ **Do the Right Thing** 1989   120 mins (cert 18)
Spike Lee confronts racial issues in part-comedy, part-drama slice of life during a day in the life of a Brooklyn community.

- -

★★★ **The Dresser** 1983   118 mins (cert PG)
Touching tale of actor-manager, *Albert Finney*, his assistant, *Tom Courtenay*, and their mutual reliance on one another.

- -

★★★ **Driving Miss Daisy** 1989   99 mins (cert U)
Pleasant, beautifully-played examination of unlikely friendship between testy old southern belle, *Jessica Tandy*, and her black chauffeur, *Morgan Freeman*. *Dan Aykroyd* provides lighter moments.

★★ **Drugstore Cowboy** 1989   100 mins (cert 18)
Matt Dillon and *Kelly Lynch* in Gus Van Sant's harsh look at the lives of a group of 1970s drug addicts.

★★★ **A Dry White Season** 1989   101 mins (cert 15)
South African apartheid forms axis on which this absorbing tale rotates. Cameo from *Marlon Brando* adds depth.

★★★ **East of Eden** 1955   119 mins (cert PG)
Steinbeck's powerful story of two brothers' rivalry for father's love. *James Dean*, in debut, exploded onto screen as the prodigal son.

★★ **Easy Rider** 1969   115 mins (cert PG)
Great, even mould-breaking in its time, but now rather dated Sixties road movie featuring *Peter Fonda*, *Jack Nicholson* and *Dennis Hopper*.

★★★ **Educating Rita** 1983   110 mins (cert 15)
Delightful, touching tale about Liverpudlian hairdresser, *Julie Walters*, taking open University degree under tutorship of *Michael Caine*.

★★★ **Edward II** 1991   90 mins (cert 18)
Derek Jarman's absorbing, idiosyncratic version of Marlowe's play about the homosexual king.

★★★ **Eight Men Out** 1984   120 mins (cert PG)
Charlie Sheen and *John Cusack* in absorbing story of Chicago White Sox baseball team who threw the World Series in 1919.

★★★ **84 Charing Cross Road** 1987   97 mins (cert U)
Anne Bancroft and *Anthony Hopkins* charm as a book buyer and book seller corresponding across the Atlantic.

★★★ **The Electric Horseman** 1979   120 mins (cert PG)
Ex-rodeo star, *Robert Redford*, steals thoroughbred horse to save them both from the scrap heap. Journalist, *Jane Fonda*, gives chase in this satire on big business.

★★ **Elenya** 1992   88 mins (cert PG)
Quiet tale of lonely Welsh girl befriending an injured German parachutist during WWII. Better suited to TV where you could take a coffee break during the slower parts.

★★★ **The Elephant Man** 1980   124 mins (cert PG)
David Lynch's sentimentalized version of the life of disfigured John Merrick expertly played by *John Hurt*.

....

★★ **The Emerald Forest** 1985   113 mins (cert 15)
Ecological drama based on true story of man's ten-year struggle to recover kidnapped son from Amazon jungle. John Boorman directed.

....

★★ **Emmanuelle** 1974   94 mins (cert 18)
Best of soft-porn movies. *Sylvia Kristel* as diplomat's wife lured into sexual deviance. At least the people look pretty.

....

★★★ **Empire of the Sun** 1987   153 mins (cert PG)
Glossy but overlong Spielberg adaptation of J G Ballard's boyhood in Japanese POW camp in WWII.

....

★★★ **Enchanted April** 1991   95 mins (cert U)
Four Edwardian ladies – *Miranda Richardson*, *Joan Plowright*, *Josie Lawrence* and *Polly Walker* – take a holiday in Italy where their lives turn around.

....

★★ **The End of the Golden Weather** 1992   103 mins (cert 12)
Young New Zealand boy believes miracles can happen – and finds they do – as he befriends a backward neighbour during a perfect summer of 1930s childhood.

....

★★ **An Enemy of the People** 1977   107 mins (cert 15)
Sincere but misguided attempt by bearded *Steve McQueen* to bring Ibsen classic to screen.

....

★★★★ **An Englishman Abroad** 1985   60 mins (cert PG)
Utterly delightful account of how actress *Carol Browne* (playing herself) met spy/traitor Guy Burgess, *Alan Bates*, in Moscow.

....

★★★ **The Entertainer** 1960   96 mins (cert 18)
Laurence Olivier superb as shabby, third-rate music hall star in fine adaptation of John Osborne play.

....

★★ **Entertaining Mister Sloane** 1970   94 mins (cert 18)
Beryl Reid outstanding in Joe Orton's kinky, and still slightly shocking, brother and sister comedy/drama.

★★ **Equinox** 1992   110 mins (cert 15)
Two brothers – a mechanic and a hoodlum – reunited by an inheritance in a thoughtful but sometimes dull story about the search for identity. *Matthew Modine* stars.

....

★★★ **The Fabulous Baker Boys** 1989   113 mins (cert 15)
Cabaret entertainers, brothers *Beau* and *Jeff Bridges*, find hidden emotions exposed by the arrival of sultry singer, *Michelle Pfeiffer*.

....

★★★ **The Falcon and the Snowman** 1985   131 mins (cert 15)
Well-made true story of two wealthy Americans, *Sean Penn* and *Timothy Hutton*, who sold state secrets to the Russians.

....

★★ **Fallen Angels** 1993   90 mins (cert 15)
Tom Cruise and *Tom Hanks* among a number of many famous faces in front of and behind the camera in a number of short crime stories – ranging from fair to dull – released on two videos.

....

★★ **The Fallen Idol** 1948   94 mins (cert 12)
Young boy worships servant accused of murdering wife in skilful adaptation of Graham Greene story.

....

★★★★ **Falling Down** 1993   115 mins (cert 18)
Michael Douglas as (fairly) ordinary Joe who snaps and rebels against a hostile Los Angeles and goes on a violent rampage. Splendidly topical and un-politically correct. *Robert Duvall* great as the policeman who tracks Douglas down.

....

★★ **Far and Away** 1992   140 mins (cert 12)
Poor Irish lad, *Tom Cruise*, and haughty noble woman, *Nicole Kidman*, run away to seek mixed fate and fortune in America. A lengthy melodrama that amounts to little.

....

★★ **Far From the Madding Crowd** 1967   175 mins (cert U)
Beautiful photography by Nicolas Roeg, skilful direction from John Schlesinger, and sharp acting from *Julie Christie* and *Alan Bates* in underrated version of Thomas Hardy novel.

....

★★★★ **A Few Good Men** 1992   138 mins (cert 15)
Cracking courtroom drama as *Tom Cruise* proves more than a plea bargaining lawyer when appointed to defend two marines court-martialled on a murder charge. *Jack Nicholson* is the Marine colonel, *Kevin Bacon* the prosecutor.

★★ **The Field** 1990   112 mins (cert 12)
Irishman's obsession with a piece of land leads to tragedy in a
florid drama. *Richard Harris* stars as a kind of Irish King Lear.
(King O'Leary?)

★★★ **The Fisher King** 1991   137 mins (cert 15)
Heartwarming 'bit of everything' story sees disillusioned DJ
Jeff Bridges shown value of life by down-and-out *Robin Williams*
in Terry Gilliam's delightful fantasy.

★★ **The Fool** 1990   137 mins (cert U)
Victorian drama starring *Derek Jacobi* as a clerk with amazing
double life. First-rate British cast can't quite surmount an
unconvincing story.

★★★ **Forever Young** 1992   102 mins (cert PG)
Frozen 1940s pilot, *Mel Gibson*, defrosted 50 years later and
searching for his lost love in a romantic weepie.

★★ **For Queen and Country** 1988   105 mins (cert 15)
Outstanding portrayal by *Denzel Washington* of a black soldier's
mistreatment following demobilization from British army.

★★ **For the Boys** 1991   140 mins (cert 15)
Bette Midler and *James Caan* as couple of musicians entertaining
US troops through three wars. Overblown and disappointing.

★★★ **The Four Seasons** 1981   108 mins (cert 15)
Great characterization marks *Alan Alda*'s poignant tale of the
friendship between three couples over the course of a year.

★★★ **1492: The Conquest of Paradise** 1992   155 mins (cert 15)
Beautiful, but rather dull and very long account of what
happened after Columbus, *Gerard Depardieu*, stumbled upon the
Americas. Good cast including *Sigourney Weaver* and *Armand
Assante*.

★★★ **Frances** 1982   139 mins (cert 15)
Outstanding portrayal by *Jessica Lange* of the tragic 1930s
actress, Frances Farmer.

★★★ **Frankie and Johnny** 1991   117 mins (cert 15)
Gary Marshall's bitter-sweet comedy set in a NY greasy spoon
where romance blossoms between lonely hearts *Michelle Pfeiffer*
and *Al Pacino*.

★★★ **The French Lieutenant's Woman** 1981   123 mins (cert 15)
Thoughtful adaptation of John Fowles' period novel with *Jeremy Irons* and *Meryl Streep* as both 18th-century soldier and the object of his desire and 20th-century lovers.

★★★★ **Fried Green Tomatoes
at the Whistle Stop Cafe** 1991   130 mins (cert 12)
Jessica Tandy relates tale of two young women, *Mary Stuart Masterson* and *Mary Louise Parker*, in America's deep south to *Kathy Bates* and changes her life. Looks great. Most pleasing.

★★ **The Front** 1976   95 mins (cert 15)
America's notorious Communist witch hunt forms the premise for this sharp, witty drama. *Woody Allen* as frontman for banned scriptwriters.

★★ **The Gambler** 1974   111 mins (cert 18)
Tense drama about a compulsive, self-destructive gambler expertly played by *James Caan*.

★★★★ **Gandhi** 1982   188 mins (cert PG)
Epic, Oscar-winning spectacular from Richard Attenborough about the life and death of the Indian leader. *Ben Kingsley* heads a superb cast as Gandhi.

★★ **Giant** 1956   201 mins (cert PG)
Overlong but stylish family saga about rise of Texas oil barons starring *Elizabeth Taylor*, *James Dean* and *Rock Hudson*.

★★★ **Glengarry Glen Ross** 1992   100 mins (cert 15)
Powerful character-led drama by David Mamet. Full of nail-biting tension as real estate salesmen, notably *Jack Lemmon* and *Al Pacino*, are given a week to meet their targets. *Alec Baldwin* dynamic in cameo role.

★★ **Gloria** 1980   123 mins (cert PG)
Gena Rowlands in title role of tough, savvy housewife protecting orphan boy from Mafia.

★★★★★ **Gone With the Wind** 1939   220 mins (cert U)
The classic, all-encompassing saga of the American Civil War, about which everyone gives a damn. *Vivien Leigh* and *Clark Gable* head the splendid cast.

★★★★ Goodbye Mr Chips 1939   114 mins (cert U)
Robert Donat's magnificent portrayal of a retiring school master
who has devoted his life to his boys.

....

★★★ Gorillas in the Mist 1988   129 mins (cert 15)
Biopic about Diane Fossey, who was murdered for trying to save
gorillas. Sensitively played by *Sigourney Weaver*.

....

★★★★ The Graduate 1967   105 mins (cert 15)
Dustin Hoffman in unforgettable account of graduate's journey to
adulthood (and adultery) via an affair with girlfriend's mother,
Anne Bancroft.

....

★★★ Grand Canyon 1992   134 mins (cert 15)
Steve Martin, *Kevin Kline* and *Danny Glover* lead well-written
social drama about problems of living in modern, violent LA.

....

★★★★ Grand Hotel 1932   115 mins (cert U)
Berlin hotel provides backdrop for excellent character study of
guests: *Greta Garbo*, *Joan Crawford*, *John* and *Lionel Barrymore*.
Often copied but the format works best here.

....

★★★★ The Grapes of Wrath 1940   128 mins (cert PG)
Compelling Steinbeck tale of workers' migration to California
during the Depression. Beautifully acted by *Henry Fonda*.

....

★ Great Balls of Fire! 1989   107 mins (cert 15)
Dennis Quaid is always watchable as the legendary rocker Jerry
Lee Lewis but the script and direction continually let him down.

....

★★ The Grifters 1990   119 mins (cert 18)
Dark story of a thieving mother, *Anjelica Huston*, and her
conman son, *John Cusack*, never quite finds its feet.

....

★★ Guilty by Suspicion 1991   105 mins (cert 15)
Rather heavy-handed account of the Hollywood victims of the
1950s Un-American Activities Committee. *Robert De Niro* as
chief suspect.

....

★★ Gypsy 1962   149 mins (cert 12)
Natalie Wood and *Rosalind Russell* star in entertaining biography
of stripper Gypsy Rose Lee and her mum.

★★★ **Hamlet** 1948 142 mins (cert U)
Masterly performance in the title role by *Laurence Oliver*, who also directed. Great supporting cast.

....

★★★ **Hamlet** 1991 133 mins (cert U)
Franco Zeffirelli's lucid, highly accessible version of William Shakespeare's tragedy. *Mel Gibson* excels as the prince.

....

★★ **A Handful of Dust** 1988 118 mins (cert PG)
Harrowing story from Evelyn Waugh about aristocrats seeking fulfilment. Pretty to look at, disturbing to watch.

....

★ **Hangin' with the Homeboys** 1991 90 mins (cert 15)
Odd adventures of mixed ethnic trio on a big night out in Manhattan.

....

★ **Havana** 1990 145 mins (cert 15)
Cuban politics form basis of rather drab 'Casablanca' rip-off. *Robert Redford*, *Raul Julia* and *Alan Arkin* all deserve better.

....

★★ **Heartburn** 1986 109 mins (cert 15)
Formidable cast, *Meryl Streep* and *Jack Nicholson*, try to cope with marital problems but result disappoints.

....

★★ **Heat and Dust** 1983 130 mins (cert 15)
Merchant Ivory story of two Englishwomen, *Greta Scacchi* and *Julie Christie*, from two eras immersed in mystery and romance of India.

....

★★★ **Heathers** 1989 103 mins (cert 18)
Christian Slater and *Winona Ryder* sparkle in this sharp black comedy about adolescence and high school politics.

....

★★ **Henry and June** 1990 136 mins (cert 18)
Earnest and strangely dull version of Henry Miller's lusty relationship with Anais Nin. With *Fred Ward* and *Uma Thurman*.

....

★★★★ **Henry V** 1944 137 mins (cert U)
Laurence Olivier's stirring, colourful pageant ideally suited to its time and the nation's celebration of coming victory.

....

★★★★ **Henry V** 1989 135 mins (cert PG)
Kenneth Branagh's superb, gritty contrast to Olivier's version. Olivier's troops were the guards, Branagh's the SAS.

★★ **Hoffa** 1992   140 mins (cert 15)
Jack Nicholson as the dubious 1950s union boss who may or may not have had close dealings with the Mafia and who died mysteriously. *Danny DeVito* is his sidekick and director in a film that never quite works.

....

★ **Homer and Eddie** 1990   99 mins (cert 15)
Bleakish hotch-potch plot about an escaped mental patient, *Whoopi Goldberg*, offering help to brain-damaged *James Belushi*.

....

★★★★ **Howards End** 1992   140 mins (cert PG)
Anthony Hopkins and Oscar-winner *Emma Thompson* lead in this beautifully-played, gorgeous-looking version of E M Forster's novel.

....

★★★★ **The Hunchback of Notre Dame** 1939   115 mins (cert PG)
The portrayal of the bell-ringing cripple by *Charles Laughton* is a tour-de-force. Remarkably touching.

....

★★★★ **The Hustler** 1961   135 mins (cert 18)
Paul Newman at his best as a hungry young pool shark taking on the formidable Minnesota Fats, *Jackie Gleason*. Riveting and almost unbearably tense.

....

★★★★ **If . . .** 1969   111 mins (cert 15)
Savage – if dated – satire on the British school and class system. Surreal violence originally earned it an 'X' (18) certificate.

....

★★ **Indian Runner** 1991   126 mins (cert 15)
Sean Penn's glum, but not unimpressive, directorial debut about two brothers on opposite sides of the law.

....

★★★ **Inherit the Wind** 1960   127 mins (cert U)
Scathing examination of 1925 prosecution of American teacher propounding Darwinian theories. *Spencer Tracy* immaculate as defence attorney.

....

★ **The Inner Circle** 1992   134 mins (cert 15)
Tom Hulce stars as Stalin's cinema projectionist surviving – just about – the terrors of the regime. First film ever to go inside the KGB headquarters – even if it was just the lobby.

....

★★★ **The Inn of the Sixth Happiness** 1958   159 mins (cert U)
Touching biography of missionary Gladys Aylwood, played by *Ingrid Bergman*, who trekked through war-torn China with refugee children.

★★★ **Intersection** 1993   107 mins (cert 15)
Classic eternal triangle set on a collision course in romantic
drama with *Sharon Stone* and *Richard Gere*. *Lolita Davidovich* plays
the mistress.

★★★★★ **In the Name of the Father** 1993   135 mins (cert 15)
Overwhelming performance by *Daniel Day-Lewis* as one of the
wrongfully imprisoned 'Guildford Four'. Righteously angry,
wickedly funny and a superb piece of filmmaking.

★★ **Ironweed** 1987   144 mins (cert 15)
Depression-based, and depressing, drama about a couple of
alcoholic down-and-outs: *Meryl Streep* and *Jack Nicholson*.

★★ **Jacknife** 1989   98 mins (cert 15)
Post-Vietnam war trauma confronted in well-acted drama.
Robert De Niro, *Kathy Baker* and *Ed Harris* do the business.

★★ **Jack the Bear** 1993   98 mins (cert 12)
Danny DeVito as a single father trying to raise two young sons.
Trouble comes when the youngest is kidnapped by local weirdo.
Uncomfortable balance of humour and horror leaves a nasty
taste in the mouth. Ill-paced direction by DeVito.

★★★ **Jane Eyre** 1944   96 mins (cert PG)
Joan Fontaine plays Charlotte Brontë's eponymous heroine who
falls for her employer – the enigmatic Mr Rochester, played
superbly by *Orson Welles*.

★★★★ **JFK** 1992   190 mins (cert 15)
Don't let the length deter you. Oliver Stone's fascinating
examination of who killed the president is flawed but riveting.
Kevin Costner heads stellar cast.

★★ **Johnny Suede** 1991   97 mins (cert 15)
Set in 1950s with *Brad Pitt* inspired to pursue career as musician
after a pair of blue suede shoes fall on his head. Quirky story
dealing with complexities of romance.

★ **Juice** 1992   91 mins (cert 15)
A rites-of-passage story about a group of teenagers discovering
whether they have the guts (the juice) to survive on the streets
of Harlem. Tough parable about the dangers of violence.

★★ **Julia** 1977   116 mins   (cert PG)
Fine acting by *Jane Fonda* as Lillian Hellman, *Vanessa Redgrave* as
Julia, in a distinguished story of a woman's ill-fated involvement
with European resistance.

★★★ **Julius Caesar** 1953   121 mins   (cert U)
Fine adaptation and great cast, notably *Marlon Brando* as Mark
Anthony, in spectacular version of Shakespeare's play.

★★ **Jungle Fever** 1991   132 mins   (cert 18)
Spike Lee's sharp, angry look at black/white relationships and
bigotry on both sides. With *Wesley Snipes* and *Annabella Sciorra*.

★★★ **The Killing Fields** 1984   142 mins   (cert 15)
Roland Joffe's sensitive account of a news reporter's harrowing
experience during Cambodian war packs a hefty punch.

★★★ **The Killing of Sister George** 1968   138 mins   (cert 18)
Comic drama when drunken, ageing lesbian actress *Beryl Reid*
finds life and love crumbling around her.

★★★ **King of the Hill** 1993   114 mins   (cert 12)
'sex, lies and videotape' director Steven Soderbergh does the
business again with this delicious tale of a young boy escaping
poverty and loneliness in his dream world.

★★★★ **Kiss of the Spider Woman** 1985   119 mins   (cert 15)
Thoughtful, sensitive tale about understanding. *William Hurt*
plays the gay, *Raul Julia* the political activist sharing prison cell.

★★★★ **Kramer vs Kramer** 1979   105 mins   (cert PG)
Warm-hearted drama of divorced couple, *Meryl Streep* and *Dustin
Hoffman*, fighting for custody of their son.

★ **Lake Consequence** 1993   121 mins   (cert 18)
So dull it's as erotic as a limp lettuce. *Joan Severance* abandons
responsibilities and morals for a weekend of lust with *Billy Zane*
and co.

★★★ **The Last Days of Chez Nous** 1990   97 mins   (cert 15)
Director Gillian Armstrong's complex tale of the mixed-up
relationships in a Sydney household headed by middle-aged
writer *Lisa Harrow* and her French husband, *Bruno Ganz*.

★★★★ **The Last Detail** 1973   108 mins (cert 18)
Navy veterans *Jack Nicholson* and *Otis Young* escort kleptomaniac recruit *Randy Quaid* to the brig in this snappy, salty, comedy/drama.

★★★ **The Last Emperor** 1987   162 mins (cert 15)
Bernardo Bertolucci's Oscar-winning dramatization of the life of China's last imperial ruler. Vivid and colourful but over-earnest and overlong.

★★ **Last Exit to Brooklyn** 1989   102 mins (cert 18)
Vaguely repellent adaptation of Hubert Selby's notorious slice-of-life novel set in Brooklyn's seedier, more violent streets.

★★★★ **The Last Picture Show** 1971   118 mins (cert 15)
Nostalgic look at growing up in small Texas town in the 1950s. Stars *Timothy Bottoms*, *Jeff Bridges* and *Cybill Shepherd*. Great soundtrack.

★★★ **Last Tango in Paris** 1973   129 mins (cert 18)
Butter never tasted the same after Bertolucci's erotic, not to mention explicit, drama starring *Marlon Brando* and *Maria Schneider*. Infamous in its time.

★★★ **The Last Temptation of Christ** 1988   164 mins (cert 18)
Martin Scorsese's controversial and thought-provoking drama about Jesus' self doubts. Disturbing but, despite vociferous critics, definitely not blasphemous.

★★★ **Lenny** 1974   111 mins (cert 18)
Dustin Hoffman stars in this Hollywood biopic of controversial comedian Lenny Bruce. First-class performance by *Valerie Perrine* as his stripper wife.

★★★ **Let Him Have It** 1991   115 mins (cert 15)
Disturbing account of the Chris Craig/Derek Bentley murder trial and the latter's subsequent scandalous execution.

★★★★ **A Letter to Three Wives** 1949   102 mins (cert U)
Rich portrayal of three women's reactions to a letter from the town tramp who's run off with one of their husbands.

★ **Light Sleeper** 1991   103 mins (cert 15)
Susan Sarandon and *Willem Dafoe* lead this thriller set in the seedy world of drug-running.

★★★★ **The Lion in Winter** 1968   134 mins (cert 15)
Atmospheric account of power struggle between Henry II, *Peter O'Toole*, and his queen, Eleanor, *Katharine Hepburn*. Splendid performances and atmosphere.

....

★★★★ **Little Dorrit** 1988   360 mins (cert U)
A superb six-hour production of Dickens' social drama with *Alec Guinness* as the Marshalsea prison inmate. Great cast. Usually shown in two parts.

....

★★★ **Little Man Tate** 1991   99 mins (cert PG)
Jodie Foster directs and stars as the inadequate mother of an eight-year-old genius who is pulled between her and his teacher, *Dianne Wiest*.

....

★★★★ **Little Women** 1933   115 mins (cert U)
George Cukor's version of Louisa M Alcott's tale of family life, centring on the fortunes of the four daughters. *Katharine Hepburn* stars. Remade – less well and with *June Allyson* – in 1949 and, for TV, in 1978.

....

★★★ **Lolita** 1962   152 mins (cert 18)
Stanley Kubrick's rich, dark version of Vladimir Nabokov's story of the infamous nymphet. *Sue Lyon* as Lolita, *James Mason* her middle-aged victim.

....

★★★★ **The Loneliness of the Long Distance Runner** 1962   104 mins (cert 15)
Tom Courtenay first-rate as young rebel selected to represent his reform school in a race. *Michael Redgrave* co-stars.

....

★★★ **The Lonely Passion of Judith Hearne** 1987   110 mins (cert 15)
Lonely Irish spinster, *Maggie Smith*, finds repressed feelings stirred by charming American, *Bob Hoskins*. Marvellous performance by Smith.

....

★★★ **The Long Day Closes** 1991   85 mins (cert 12)
Continuing Terence Davies' autobiographical series after 'Distant Voices, Still Lives'. Leisurely, self-indulgent, but oddly fascinating. Includes the longest close-up of a piece of carpet in cinema history.

....

★★ **Longtime Companion** 1990   99 mins (cert 15)
Tactful handling of the effect of AIDS on the homosexual community in New York.

★★★ Look Back in Anger 1958   115 mins (cert 18)
Richard Burton stars in screen version of John Osborne play that changed British theatre in the 1950s. Just about as good as Burton got in the movies.

★★ Looking for Mr Goodbar 1977   136 mins (cert 18)
Glum, sordid tale about repressed young woman, *Diane Keaton*, seeking sex – and danger – in singles bar. Notable for early appearance of *Richard Gere* as the menacing stud.

★★ The Lord of the Flies 1990   95 mins (cert 15)
Aimed-at-America remake of Peter Brooks' 1963 version of William Golding's novel. Solid but pedestrian.

★★★ Lorenzo's Oil 1992   135 mins (cert 12)
Tour-de-force performance by *Susan Sarandon* as determined mother of AZT sufferer, who with husband *Nick Nolte* found a remedy for son's incurable disease. True story.

★★ Love Field 1993   101 mins (cert 15)
Deserved a cinema release. A quality tale of mixed race relationship in 1950s deep south USA between *Michelle Pfeiffer* and single father, *Dennis Haysbert*.

★ The Lover 1992   115 mins (cert 18)
Jane March, the young girl growing up – rapidly – in Vietnam. An exploitative tale of East seduces West. Only remotely interesting question is: did March and *Tony Leung* REALLY do it?

★★ Love Story 1970   100 mins (cert PG)
Famous – or notorious? – sickly sweet story about young lovers, doomed *Ali MacGraw* and *Ryan O'Neal*, heading for tragedy.

★★★ Love Streams 1984   135 mins (cert 15)
Examination by *John Cassavetes* of a couple's relationship at a tough time in their lives. Cassavetes and *Gena Rowlands* are the couple. Thoughtful but not many laughs.

★★★ Lucas 1986   96 mins (cert 15)
Charming tale of love and romance between a 14-year-old boy and a 16-year-old girl and of how their relationship affects the people around them. An engaging movie.

★★ **Mac** 1993   117 mins (cert 12)
John Turturro's over-earnest but decent directorial debut with
himself in the lead as a young builder extolling the now
apparently moribund virtues of craftsmanship.

....

★★ **Macbeth** 1971   140 mins (cert 15)
Roman Polanski directs this violent but gripping adaptation of
Shakespeare's regal play, with *Jon Finch* and *Francesca Annis*.

....

★★★ **Madame Sousatzka** 1988   116 mins (cert 15)
Shirley MacLaine as an eccentric Russian piano teacher in
London who is smitten with a desire to teach music – and the
meaning of life – to a 15-year-old Indian boy.

....

★★★ **The Magic Box** 1951   118 mins (cert U)
Every noted British actor crops up in this fascinating biopic of
William Friese-Greene, one of the inventors of the movies.

....

★★★ **Major League** 1989   107 mins (cert 15)
Bitchy woman owner plots the downfall of an already no-hoper
baseball team. Players *Tom Berenger*, *Charlie Sheen*, etc, are out to
thwart her. Light-hearted fun.

....

★★★ **Malcolm X** 1993   201 mins (cert 15)
An interminably long study of the black civil rights leader who
embraced Islam and only at the end of his life renounced
violence. *Denzel Washington* excellent in the title role. *Spike Lee*
angry and indulgent in his direction.

....

★★ **The Mambo Kings** 1992   104 mins (cert 15)
Two lusty Latino brothers – *Armand Assante* and *Antonio Banderas*
– arrive in New York from Cuba and introduce their own form of
music and dance: mambo. Okay, but should have been better.

....

★★★★ **A Man for all Seasons** 1966   120 mins (cert U)
Absorbing account of Sir Thomas More's fateful refusal to
betray the Church for his king, Henry II. *Paul Scofield* gives an
outstanding performance.

....

★★★ **The Man in the Moon** 1991   99 mins (cert PG)
Two young girls experience love and tragedy as they come of
age in southern USA.

★★★ **The Man Without a Face** 1993 114 mins (cert 12)
Mel Gibson as the man with half a face, scarred physically and
emotionally by a car crash leaving him a recluse. Until, that is,
young *Nick Stahl* asks him for help. But the township are
suspicious of the friendship.

★ **Map of the Human Heart** 1993 109 mins (cert 15)
Overpraised romantic drama spanning the formative years of
two orphans, *Jason Scott Lee* and *Anne Parillaud*, first in the
Arctic, then re-meeting in London during WWII.

★★★★ **M*A*S*H** 1970 116 mins (cert 15)
This scathing story of a US military medical unit in Korean war
spawned long-running TV series. *Donald Sutherland* and *Elliot
Gould* as the charismatic doctors.

★★★★ **Mask** 1985 120 mins (cert 15)
Eric Stoltz as the young lad disfigured by lionitis and *Cher* as his
mother, determined to give him a normal life. Moving story
based on fact.

★★ **Matewan** 1987 132 mins (cert 15)
John Sayles' thoughtful drama centring on the rebellion of the
blacks imported to break West Virginian miners' strike in 1920.

★★ **Medicine Man** 1992 105 mins (cert PG)
Sean Connery graces worthy but unconvincing ecological tale of
doctor seeking cancer cure in the rain forest. With *Lorraine
Bracco*.

★★ **Meeting Venus** 1991 119 mins (cert 12)
Glenn Close stars as a diva in a David Puttnam/Istvan Szabo
European co-production about love and language problems
during an international production of Tannhauser.

★★ **Memphis** 1991 109 mins (cert 12)
Cybill Shepherd as member of kidnap gang who begins to feel
sorry for their hostage.

★★ **Men Don't Leave** 1990 114 mins (cert 15)
Penniless widow, *Jessica Lange*, struggles to bring up two young
sons alone. A sort of touching, amusing soap opera, nicely
played.

★★★ **A Midnight Clear** 1991   108 mins (cert 15)
Six GIs in the front line in 1944 learn what war is about. Young
talented cast includes *Peter Berg*, *Kevin Dillon*, *Ethan Hawke* and
Arye Gross. Strong, simple, anti-war movie.

....

★★★★ **Midnight Express** 1978   121 mins (cert 18)
Harrowing version of Billy Hayes' experiences in Turkish jail.
Phenomenally powerful direction by Alan Parker.

....

★★★ **Millers Crossing** 1990   115 mins (cert 18)
Complex gangster movie of two Irish American hoods, *Albert
Finney* and *Gabriel Byrne*, at loggerheads over a woman.

....

★★ **The Misfits** 1961   124 mins (cert PG)
Marilyn Monroe and *Clark Gable* as a lonely, mismatched couple
drawn to each other during mustang hunt in Nevada desert.
Gable's last film.

....

★★ **Miss Firecracker** 1989   103 mins (cert PG)
Low-key comedy of Mississippi small-town life. *Holly Hunter* very
good as lonely girl seeking love and self-esteem.

....

★★ **The Mission** 1983   125 mins (cert PG)
Roland Joffe's visually impressive but overly complex
drama/tragedy about a Jesuit mission to the heart of South
America. *Robert De Niro* and *Jeremy Irons* star.

....

★★★★ **Mississippi Burning** 1988   127 mins (cert 18)
Alan Parker's controversial but powerful account of the
disappearance of three 1960s civil rights workers in deep south
USA.

....

★★ **Mississippi Masala** 1991   114 mins (cert 15)
Denzel Washington in story of love and bigotry between American
blacks and expatriate Ugandan Asians.

....

★★ **Mo' Better Blues** 1990   129 mins (cert 15)
Spike Lee's surprisingly sentimental look at a jazz musician,
Denzel Washington, forced to choose between his music and the
women in his life.

....

★★ **The Moderns** 1988   126 mins (cert 15)
Keith Carradine as art forger in beautiful but bland look at the
1920s arty set in Paris.

★★ **The Molly Maguires** 1970   119 mins (cert PG)
Secret informer *Richard Harris* infiltrates secret 1870s group of
Pennsylvanian miners, headed by *Sean Connery*, who use
terrorism to seek better conditions.

★★ **Mommie Dearest** 1981   124 mins (cert 15)
Faye Dunaway hams it up as Joan Crawford in a film based on
the book by Crawford's daughter which exposed Joanie as a
monster mum.

★★ **Mo' Money** 1991   90 mins (cert 15)
Comedy with a violent edge which spills over into humour
about two brothers trying to rip off a gang of crooks. *Damon
Wayans* and *Marlon Wayans* star.

★★★ **A Month in the Country** 1987   96 mins (cert PG)
Post-WWI drama about two scarred soldiers, *Colin Firth* and
Kenneth Branagh, recovering from wartime horrors in Yorkshire
village. So authentic you can smell the new-mown hay.

★★ **Mountains of the Moon** 1990   135 mins (cert 15)
Rival Victorian explorers, *Patrick Bergin* and *Iain Glen*, vie with
each other to trace the source of the Nile. A slightly odd epic
that doesn't quite add up.

★★★★ **Mrs Miniver** 1942   134 mins (cert U)
Greer Garson tries to keep body, soul and family together in face
of encroaching WWII. Marvellous propaganda movie to
encourage US involvement in war.

★★★★ **Mr Smith Goes to Washington** 1939   130 mins (cert U)
An innocent school teacher, *James Stewart*, finds nothing but
corruption in US Senate and bravely fights to expose it in
Capra's splendid, famous movie.

★★★ **Murder in Mississippi** 1990   123 mins (cert 18)
Alternative account of three civil rights workers murdered in
1964. Factually more accurate than 'Mississippi Burning'.

★★★★ **The Music Box** 1989   126 mins (cert 15)
Costa-Gavras' powerful, much underrated story of a lawyer,
Jessica Lange, defending her father, *Armin Mueller-Stahl*, who is
accused of wartime atrocities.

★★★ **My Beautiful Launderette** 1985   97 mins (cert 15)
Sensitive examination of racism in London's East End, as experienced by Pakistani and his gay white lover. First starring role for *Daniel Day-Lewis*.

★★★★ **My Left Foot** 1989   98 mins (cert PG)
Uplifting account of the life of Christy Brown, magnificently played by *Daniel Day-Lewis*, who, despite crippling cerebral palsy, became a celebrated writer.

★★ **My Own Private Idaho** 1991   105 mins (cert 18)
Two gay hustlers, *Keanu Reeves* and the late *River Phoenix*, go to Rome to find Phoenix's mother. A bizarre effort this, mixing fantasy and realism and with little apparent idea of where it's going.

★ **The Mystery of Edwin Drood** 1992   97 mins (cert 15)
Disappointing, anachronistic version of Dickens' unfinished novel. *Robert Powell* almost saves it but not quite.

★★★ **Mystic Pizza** 1988   104 mins (cert 15)
Sweetly appealing study of the hopes, dreams and amorous adventures of three young girls; co-stars *Julia Roberts* in an early role.

★★ **Naked Lunch** 1992   110 mins (cert 18)
Be warned – don't eat when watching this. Some of the effects are stomach-churning. Bold but unsuccessful attempt to film William Burrough's unfilmable book. *Peter Weller*, *Judy Davis* and *Julian Sands* try hard under David Cronenberg's offbeat direction.

★★★ **The Natural** 1984   134 mins (cert PG)
Curious but watchable period piece with *Robert Redford* as an exceptionally – perhaps supernaturally – gifted baseball player.

★ **Necessary Roughness** 1991   108 mins (cert 12)
Juvenile nonsense in which farmer *Scott Bakula* goes back to college to save its football team. Predictable and feeble.

★★★ **Network** 1976   120 mins (cert PG)
Sidney Lumet's effective satire of the TV world. *Peter Finch* won a posthumous Oscar in the starring role.

★★★ New York Stories 1989   125 mins (cert 15)
A trilogy of short films from Woody Allen (fine), Martin
Scorsese (very good) and Francis Coppola (forget it).

★★★ Nicholas and Alexandra 1971   183 mins (cert PG)
Overblown epic depicting events leading to Russian Revolution
and its effect on Tsar Nicholas, *Michael Jayston*, and family.

★★★ Night on Earth 1992   129 mins (cert 15)
Five stories based in five taxi cabs in five cities. Poignant, funny
and bizarre featuring the likes of *Winona Ryder*, *Rosie Perez*,
Beatrice Dalle and *Armin Mueller-Stahl*.

★★ The Night We Never Met 1993   109 mins (cert 18)
Case of mistaken identities with *Anabella Sciorra*, *Matthew
Broderick* and *Kevin Anderson*.

★★ 9½ Weeks 1986   116 mins (cert 18)
Explicit sexual activity between *Mickey Rourke* and *Kim Basinger*
but a tedious story takes the edge off erotica.

★★★ No Highway 1951   98 mins (cert U)
Halfway over the Atlantic a plane – designed by *James Stewart* –
is told it's going to crash with *Marlene Dietrich* and *Glynis Johns*
on board.

★★★ Norma Rae 1979   114 mins (cert PG)
Sally Field winning her first Oscar as the Southern mill worker
organising a union. *Beau Bridges* as her husband.

★★★ No Surrender 1985   100 mins (cert 15)
Biting social satire set in a Northern nightclub where two sets
of rival old folks come into riotous conflict.

★★ Not Without My Daughter 1991   115 mins (cert 12)
Sentimental but true story of an American mother, *Sally Field*,
attempting to recover her daughter held in Iran by father,
Alfred Molina.

★★★★ Now, Voyager 1942   117 mins (cert PG)
A gloriously weepy melodrama with spinster, *Betie Davis*,
embarked on anguished affair with married man, *Paul Heinreid*.

★★★★ **The Nun's Story** 1959   151 mins (cert U)
Audrey Hepburn as nun in the Belgian Congo rebelling against her vows. With *Peter Finch*, *Edith Evans* and *Dame Peggy Ashcroft*.

★★★ **An Officer and a Gentleman** 1982   124 mins (cert 15)
Corny but well-acted story of love affair between officer-cadet, *Richard Gere*, and factory girl, *Debra Winger*.

★★★ **Of Mice and Men** 1992   110 mins (cert PG)
Beautiful remake of Steinbeck's touching tale. *Gary Sinise* is outstanding as George, the itinerant farm labourer trying to find work for himself and the simple Lennie, *John Malkovich*.

★★ **Old Gringo** 1989   119 mins (cert 15)
The Mexican revolution of 1910 is the setting for spinster, *Jane Fonda*, and her adventures with journalist, *Gregory Peck*, and revolutionary, *Jimmy Smits*.

★★★ **The Old Lady Who Walked in the Sea** 1991   95 mins (cert 18)
Jeanne Moreau glorious as old woman carrying out series of jewel robberies with the help of her devoted old friend while playing him off against her toy-boy lover.

★★★★ **Oliver Twist** 1948   116 mins (cert U)
Alec Guinness is brilliant as Fagin in the matchless David Lean version of Dickens' saga.

★★ **Once Around** 1991   110 mins (cert 15)
Italian-American family's life turned around when the daughter falls for an unsuitable suitor. With *Holly Hunter*, *Richard Dreyfuss*, *Danny Aiello* and *Laura San Giacomo*.

★★★★ **One Flew Over the Cuckoo's Nest** 1975   134 mins (cert 18)
Multi-Oscar winner by Milos Forman celebrates triumph of the individual over the system. *Jack Nicholson* excellent as are all the cast.

★★★ **On Golden Pond** 1981   109 mins (cert PG)
Sentimental tale of family reconciliation made more poignant for featuring the estranged *Jane* and *Henry Fonda* – his last film – and *Katherine Hepburn*.

★★★ **Only Angels Have Wings** 1939   121 mins (cert U)
Cary Grant as boss of an airfreight company in the Andes where (continually) hazardous weather conditions and showgirl *Jean Arthur* create tension.

★★★★ **On the Waterfront** 1954   108 mins (cert PG)
Corruption amongst dock workers inspires ex-boxer, *Marlon Brando*, to fight against oppression in Elia Kazan's gripping film.

....

★★★ **Ordinary People** 1980   124 mins (cert 15)
A poignant tale of the effect of a boy's suicide on his family. With *Donald Sutherland* and *Mary Tyler Moore*. Robert Redford won the Oscar for his direction.

....

★★★ **Orlando** 1993   93 mins (cert PG)
Tilda Swinton as Virginia Woolf's androgynous heroine who lives 400 years. *Billy Zane* and *Quentin Crisp* in support. A little delight.

....

★★ **An Outcast of the Islands** 1951   102 mins (cert PG)
Study of moral decay. *Ralph Richardson* and *Trevor Howard* as hunter and hunted on Malayan island.

....

★★★ **Out of Africa** 1985   161 mins (cert PG)
Great cast – *Robert Redford* and *Meryl Streep* – great scenery, but mildly disappointing love story.

....

★★ **Paradise** 1992   111 mins (cert 12)
Melanie Griffith and *Don Johnson* as a married couple forced to confront their problems when young *Elijah Wood* comes to stay. Pretty but uninvolving.

....

★★ **Paris, Texas** 1984   150 mins (cert 15)
Wim Wenders' much-praised but ultimately unsatisfying Texan road movie. *Harry Dean Stanton* and *Nastassja Kinski* star.

....

★★★ **A Passage to India** 1984   163 mins (cert PG)
David Lean's sumptuous adaptation of E M Forster's drama of East/West culture clash in 1920s India. *Judy Davis* fine, but *Alec Guinness* miscast.

....

★★ **Passion Fish** 1993   135 mins (cert 15)
Story of burgeoning friendship between newly paralysed *Mary McDonnell* and home help *Alfre Woodard* with problems of her own. Pleasing story set against the beautiful backdrop of America's deep south.

....

★★★★ **The Piano** 1993   120 mins (cert 15)
Holly Hunter as the 19th-century mute mail-order bride shipped to New Zealand. *Harvey Keitel* co-stars in fascinating, unusual story of sexual passion.

★★★ **Picnic at Hanging Rock** 1975   112 mins (cert 18)
Gripping account of events leading to eerie disappearance of
Australian schoolgirls and their teacher during school outing.

★★ **Places in the Heart** 1984   111 mins (cert PG)
Plucky *Sally Field* as a farmer's widow struggling during
Depression to keep her Texas farm.

★★ **The Playboys** 1992   108 mins (cert 12)
Albert Finney and travelling player *Aidan Quinn* vie for the hand
of unmarried mother *Robin Wright* in a 1950s Irish village.
Pleasing tale with good performances.

★★★ **Postcards from the Edge** 1991   104 mins (cert 15)
Hollywood portrayal of actress, *Meryl Streep*, the drug-addicted
daughter of overshadowing famous mother, *Shirley MacLaine*. In
parts very funny, in others a bit off the mark.

★★ **The Power of One** 1992   127 mins (cert 12)
Young lad growing up in South Africa in WWII. New slant on
the race theme. Simplistic but pleasing.

★★★ **Prick Up Your Ears** 1987   110 mins (cert 18)
Gary Oldman very impressive as British playwright Joe Orton;
Alfred Molina plays his lover who ultimately kills him.

★★ **Pride and Prejudice** 1940   116 mins (cert U)
This pleasing, though hardly faithful version of Jane Austen's
delightful romance stars *Greer Garson* and *Laurence Olivier*.

★★ **The Prince of Tides** 1992   131 mins (cert 15)
Barbra Streisand's melodramatic love story. *Nick Nolte* is the man
with a disturbed past; Streisand the psychiatrist making him
confront it.

★★ **Proof** 1991   90 mins (cert 15)
Distrustful blind man uses photography to ensure people tell
him the truth in strangely absorbing Australian story.

★★ **Prospero's Books** 1991   120 mins (cert 15)
Myriad of impressive visuals but style better than content in
Peter Greenaway's version of 'The Tempest'.

★★ **Pumping Iron** 1977   85 mins (cert 12)
Only mentioned since it's amusing for an early sight of Mr
Universe – *Arnold Schwarzenegger*. Bet he didn't demand a
$15 million fee in those days.

★★★★ **Queen Christina** 1933   101 mins (cert U)
Probably *Greta Garbo*'s best dramatic role as Swedish queen
relinquishing throne for love.

★★★ **The Quiet Man** 1952   131 mins (cert U)
Sentimental, romanticized vehicle for *John Wayne* as ex-boxer
settling in Irish village full of usual stereotypes. Ludicrous fight
sequence but pleasing nonetheless.

★ **The Rachel Papers** 1989   95 mins (cert 18)
Maladroit attempt at modern comedy of manners based on the
Martin Amis novel.

★★★★ **Raging Bull** 1980   129 mins (cert 18)
Martin Scorsese's study of boxing champion Jake La Motta.
Brilliant performance from *Robert De Niro* helps make this one
of the best films of the 1980s.

★★ **Ragtime** 1981   155 mins (cert 18)
Socially aware drama of racism in turn-of-century America.
Notable for inducing *James Cagney* out of twenty-year
retirement.

★★★ **Rain Man** 1988   133 mins (cert 15)
Relationship of autistic savant, *Dustin Hoffman*, and initially
ruthless brother, *Tom Cruise*. Two fine performances, especially
by Cruise.

★★ **Rambling Rose** 1991   112 mins (cert 15)
Family life in 1930s disrupted by arrival of promiscuous child of
nature, *Laura Dern*, in home of *Robert Duvall* and *Diane Ladd*.

★★★ **Rebel Without a Cause** 1955   111 mins (cert PG)
James Dean's angry young man looks dated now but still bears
emotional resonance of teenage alienation.

★★★ **Reds** 1981   196 mins (cert 15)
Warren Beatty's Oscar-winning directorial debut about American
journalist's espousal of communism. Beatty and *Diane Keaton* star.

★★★★ **The Red Shoes** 1948　　　　　　　　134 mins　(cert U)
Powell and Pressburger's marvellous, innovative tale about the
staging of a ballet and a young dancer, *Moira Shearer*, torn
between two men.

★★ **Regarding Henry** 1991　　　　　　　　107 mins　(cert 12)
Harrison Ford in an unconvincing story about a ruthless lawyer
whose attitude to family and work changes drastically after he's
shot.

★★★★ **The Remains of the Day** 1993　　　　　138 mins　(cert U)
Merchant Ivory stick faithfully to the book wherein class-
conscious butler, *Anthony Hopkins*, reflects on his life of missed
opportunities. Hopkins outstanding; well supported by *Emma
Thompson*.

★★★ **Reversal of Fortune** 1990　　　　　　111 mins　(cert 15)
Impeccable performance by *Jeremy Irons* as Claus Von Bulow,
accused of trying to murder his wealthy wife, *Glenn Close*. Based
on a true story.

★★★★ **Richard III** 1955　　　　　　　　　161 mins　(cert U)
Laurence Olivier's performance as Crookback scared generations
of actors away from the role. Good, if stagy, production.

★★ **Rich in Love** 1993　　　　　　　　　105 mins　(cert PG)
A nine-year-old girl tries to hold her family together when her
mother walks out. *Albert Finney* is the deserted husband picking
up pieces of his life. Gentle family drama set against
spectacular back drop of deep south USA.

★★ **The River** 1984　　　　　　　　　　122 mins　(cert PG)
Mel Gibson and *Sissy Spacek* as Tennessee farmers who find their
way of life is under threat. Intelligent, sombre drama.

★★ **A River Runs Through It** 1992　　　　　123 mins　(cert PG)
Gentle, non-eventful tale of father *Tom Skerritt*'s relationship
with his two very different sons, *Brad Pitt* and *Craig Sheffer*.
Robert Redford narrates and directs.

★★★ **Robin and Marian** 1976　　　　　　　107 mins　(cert PG)
Sean Connery and *Audrey Hepburn* as the now-ageing outlaws in a
splendid period piece of such atmosphere you can smell it.

★★★ **The Rocking Horse Winner** 1950   90 mins (cert 15)
Unusual, moving D H Lawrence story of a small boy with the
knack of picking racetrack winners. Fine performances.

★★★ **Roger & Me** 1989   91 mins (cert 15)
Michael Moore's extraordinary documentary exposes the
despair of a Michigan town when General Motors moved out.

★★★ **Roman Holiday** 1953   118 mins (cert U)
Touching, tender romance between runaway princess, *Audrey
Hepburn*, and journalist, *Gregory Peck*.

★★★ **Romero** 1989   101 mins (cert 15)
Raul Julia stars in absorbing, though sometimes vague attempt
to tell the story of the El Salvador archbishop/revolutionary who
was assassinated in 1980.

★★★ **A Room With a View** 1985   115 mins (cert PG)
Beautiful adaptation of E M Forster's Italian-based tale of
English manners. Photography and British cast superb.

★★ **Rosalie Goes Shopping** 1989   93 mins (cert 15)
Comic satire on consumerism. *Marianne Sagebrecht* as a bored
housewife who mounts up huge shopping bill on credit cards.

★★★ **Running on Empty** 1988   117 mins (cert 15)
Christine Lahti and *Judd Hirsch*, on the run for years from the FBI
as wanted terrorists, find their safety threatened when their
son, *River Phoenix*, is offered a music scholarship.

★★ **Rush** 1992   120 mins (cert 18)
Hard-hitting drama of narcotics cops, *Jennifer Jason Leigh* and
Jason Patric, working undercover and becoming addicts
themselves.

★★★ **Ryan's Daughter** 1970   206 mins (cert 15)
David Lean's overblown – but underrated – story of a young
wife, *Sara Miles*, and her love affair with a shell-shocked British
soldier in a small Irish community.

★★★ **Salaam Bombay!** 1988   113 mins (cert 15)
Vivid characterization marks potent Indian tale of a young
boy's struggle to survive on the streets of Bombay.

★★★ **Salvador** 1986   123 mins (cert 18)
Oliver Stone's powerful, sobering account of the experiences of
journalist Richard Boyle – *James Woods* – in war-torn El Salvador.

★★ **Same Time Next Year** 1978   119 mins (cert 15)
Sweet story of a couple, *Ellen Burstyn* and *Alan Alda*, who meet
for a brief adulterous affair every year. Low-key but charming.

★★★ **Saturday Night and Sunday Morning** 1960   89 mins (cert 15)
Albert Finney's first starring role as the angry young man in Alan
Sillitoe's gritty, evocative study of working-class life.

★★★ **Scandal** 1989   114 mins (cert 18)
Absorbing examination of the Profumo Affair which brought
down the British government in the 1960s. Lovely performances
by *John Hurt*, *Joanne Whalley-Kilmer* and *Bridget Fonda*.

★★★ **Scent of a Woman** 1992   156 mins (cert 15)
Al Pacino is splendid as the blind war veteran who hires preppy
Chris O'Donnell to be his eyes during one final, blow-out weekend
in New York.

★★★★ **Secret Honor** 1984   90 mins (cert 15)
Philip Baker Hall excels in this astonishing one-man show
directed by Robert Altman and based on the alleged ravings of
a suicidal Richard Nixon. Really chilling stuff.

★★ **The Secret of My Success** 1987   110 mins (cert PG)
Michael J Fox heads for the big city and finds corruption in the
workplace, streets and bedroom.

★★★★ **The Servant** 1963   116 mins (cert 18)
Sexual overtones help to create atmosphere and tension as *Dirk
Bogarde*, the cunning manservant, gradually becomes the master
of his employer, *James Fox*.

★★★★ **sex, lies and videotape** 1989   100 mins (cert 18)
Astonishing directorial debut of Steven Soderbergh with story
of small-town marital and extra-marital relationships. Fine cast
headed by *James Spader* and *Andie MacDowell*.

★★★ **Shampoo** 1975   110 mins (cert 18)
Hip, sexy and very Seventies satire of Californian morals.
Warren Beatty stars as the hairdresser servicing his demanding
clientele, *Julie Christie* and *Goldie Hawn* among them.

★★ **She-Devil** 1991　　　　　　　　99 mins (cert 15)
Silly adaptation of Fay Weldon's black and bleak comedy of a
fat woman's revenge, which misses the entire point. *Roseanne
Barr* is the fat woman, *Meryl Streep* the thin.

....

★★ **The Sheltering Sky** 1990　　　　　138 mins (cert 18)
Drab, period reconstruction of Paul Bowle's famous novel about
a couple, *John Malkovich* and *Debra Winger*, discovering North
Africa after WWII.

....

★★★★ **Shirley Valentine** 1989　　　　　109 mins (cert 15)
Delightful, gentle Willy Russell story with *Pauline Collins* as the
bored Liverpudlian housewife who ups to a Greek island in
search of romance.

....

★★★★ **The Shooting Party** 1984　　　　　96 mins (cert 15)
Deeply moving examination of class and culture centring on a
weekend shooting party in 1913. *James Mason* brilliant in his
penultimate role.

....

★★★★★ **Short Cuts** 1993　　　　　　　185 mins (cert 18)
Robert Altman takes the pick of Hollywood's actors and a
bunch of stories and knits them all together in this gloriously
inspired movie.

....

★★★ **Shout** 1991　　　　　　　　　85 mins (cert PG)
Quiet but appealing story about the effect of a music teacher –
John Travolta – on a troubled teenager in reform school.

....

★★★ **Silas Marner** 1985　　　　　　　92 mins (cert PG)
Decent adaptation of the classic novel. *Ben Kingsley* as miserly
Marner, the weaver whose life is changed by an adopted child.

....

★★★ **Silkwood** 1983　　　　　　　　131 mins (cert 15)
Meryl Streep as Karen Silkwood, who uncovered a dangerous
secret at a nuclear plant and mysteriously died; *Cher* as her best
friend. An important, disturbing film.

....

★★★ **Singles** 1992　　　　　　　　　99 mins (cert 12)
Group of late twentysomethings wanting to settle down and
looking for Mr (or Mrs) Right. With *Bridget Fonda*, *Matt Dillon*,
Kyra Sedgwick and many others.

★★★★ **The Six Wives of Henry VIII** 1972　　541 mins (cert PG)
Scintillating TV drama starring *Keith Michell*, excellent as the
ambitious young king growing into a disillusioned, tyrannical
monarch.

★ **Slaves of New York** 1989　　125 mins (cert 15)
Sadly disappointing screen version (directed by James Ivory) of
Tama Janowitz's once-trendy book about Manhattan's arty set.

★★★ **Sommersby** 1992　　112 mins (cert 15)
After the American Civil War *Richard Gere* returns home to wife
Jodie Foster – but is he the man who went away? Moving story
though the French version, 'The Return of Martin Guerre', is
better.

★★★ **Sophie's Choice** 1982　　151 mins (cert 15)
Meryl Streep gives a heartrending performance as the survivor of
a Nazi concentration camp struggling to find happiness in
America.

★★ **Stand and Deliver** 1987　　104 mins (cert 15)
Gentle, based-on-fact drama of Hispanic headmaster adopting
unorthodox methods to ensure his drug-pushing, gang-member
pupils win qualifications.

★★★ **Stand By Me** 1986　　87 mins (cert 15)
Affectionate, nostalgic glimpse of boyhood friendship in 1950s
America, based on Stephen King's rites-of-passage story. *River
Phoenix* splendid in the leading role.

★★ **Stanley and Iris** 1990　　104 mins (cert 15)
Hard-up widow *Jane Fonda* finds love when teaching the dyslexic
Robert De Niro to read. Sincerely meant but dullish stuff.

★★★ **Steel Magnolias** 1989　　117 mins (cert 15)
Bittersweet comedy following the lives of female friends in a
small Louisiana town. Nice acting from a cast that includes
Julia Roberts, *Shirley MacLaine* and *Sally Field*.

★★ **Stella** 1989　　114 mins (cert 15)
Presence of *Bette Midler*, sassy in the title role, almost saves
sentimental story of a woman's lone fight to raise her daughter
in a remake of 'Stella Dallas'. Almost.

★★★ **St Elmo's Fire** 1985   108 mins (cert 15)
Entertaining Brat Packers movie with *Emilio Estevez*, *Judd Nelson*
and *Demi Moore* finding that life after college can be a bitch.

★★ **Stepping Out** 1991   105 mins (cert PG)
Liza Minnelli runs a tap-dance class of unfulfilled women and
one man. All need the help and friendship the class provides.
Julie Walters lightens tone.

★★ **Straight Out of Brooklyn** 1991   83 mins (cert 15)
A crime-ridden black area of NY is the setting for this bleak
drama of a young lad in a downward spiral and unable to break
out of social rut.

★★★ **Strapless** 1989   99 mins (cert 15)
David Hare directed his own story of an American doctor, *Blair
Brown*, who marries on a whim but soon regrets it. Good
performances by Brown and *Bridget Fonda*.

★★★★ **A Streetcar Named Desire** 1951   122 mins (cert 18)
Powerful Tennesse Williams melodrama. Great performances
by Oscar-winning *Vivien Leigh*, *Kim Hunter*, *Karl Malden* and
especially by *Marlon Brando* who, alone, missed an Oscar. Why?

★★★★★ **Sunset Boulevard** 1950   110 mins (cert PG)
Billy Wilder's subtly vicious indictment of Hollywood. *William
Holden* as young writer tragically involved with has-been movie
star, *Gloria Swanson*.

★★★ **Swann in Love** 1984   111 mins (cert 18)
Tightly-squeezed excerpt from Proust's 'Remembrance of
Things Past'. *Jeremy Irons* is the French aristocrat consumed by
passion for social-climbing *Ornella Muti*.

★★★ **Sweetie** 1989   100 mins (cert 15)
Jane Campion's first – strange – film, a tragi-comedy about two
oddball sisters Down Under. Unusual and imaginative, though
it doesn't always hit the mark.

★★ **Swing Kids** 1993   114 mins (cert 15)
Germany, 1939, and a group of kids who embrace the swing/jazz
culture oppose the Nazis. Could have been fascinating but cops
out. With *Robert Sean Leonard*, *Christian Bale* and *Kenneth Branagh*
(who kept his name off the credits).

★★★ **Talk Radio** 1988   108 mins (cert 18)
Eric Bogosian as radio talk-show host whose controversial style
wins notoriety and worse in Oliver Stone's grim, moral tale.

....

★★★★ **Taxi Driver** 1976   114 mins (cert 18)
Martin Scorsese's disturbing but brilliant view of ultra-violent
New York seen through the eyes of a psychotic cabbie, *Robert
De Niro*. Also stars a young *Jodie Foster*.

....

★★★ **Tender Mercies** 1983   90 mins (cert PG)
Poignant performance from *Robert Duvall* as a down-at-heel
country singer rebuilding his life around young widow, *Tess
Harper*, and her son.

....

★★★ **Terms of Endearment** 1983   132 mins (cert 15)
Sub-plot involving *Jack Nicholson* and *Shirley MacLaine* is funny
but sentimentality of main plot where daughter, *Debra Winger*,
is dying from cancer, sticks in the throat.

....

★★ **Texasville** 1990   126 mins (cert 15)
Disappointing follow-up to 'The Last Picture Show', resuming
life stories of *Jeff Bridges*, *Cybill Shepherd*, *Timothy Bottoms* and
Randy Quaid in the 1980s.

....

★★★★ **These Foolish Things** 1990   102 mins (cert PG)
Bertrand Tavernier's bittersweet story of the relationship
between an ailing father, *Dirk Bogarde*, and his daughter, *Jane
Birkin*. Beautifully played.

....

★★★★ **They Shoot Horses, Don't They?** 1969   129 mins (cert 15)
Bleak view of America during the Depression in a story of
marathon dancing contests which sometimes lasted for weeks.
Jane Fonda stars.

....

★★★★★ **The Third Man** 1949   100 mins (cert PG)
Carol Reed's superb thriller set in post-war Vienna with *Joseph
Cotten* as the naive American searching for his mysterious
friend, *Orson Welles*. A movie classic.

....

★★ **This Boy's Life** 1993   115 mins (cert PG)
Bland, yet hard-to-believe, coming-of-age story with a 'so what?'
ending. *Robert De Niro* is the sadistic stepfather, *Ellen Barkin* the
mother and *Leonardo DiCaprio* the boy.

★★★ **The Three Faces of Eve** 1957   91 mins (cert 15)
Powerful performance by *Joanne Woodward* as a schizophrenic
with three diverse lives.

★★★ **To Kill a Mockingbird** 1962   129 mins (cert PG)
Rich drama based in deep south USA, concentrating upon
family of a lawyer, *Gregory Peck*, defending a black accused
of rape.

★★★ **Torch Song Trilogy** 1988   119 mins (cert 15)
Evocative and emotional comedy/drama told in three parts
about a homosexual, *Harvey Fierstein*, coming to terms with his
problems.

★★ **To Sir With Love** 1967   105 mins (cert PG)
Highly competent account of black school teacher, *Sidney Poitier*,
earning respect and devotion of unruly pupils.

★★★★ **The Treasure of the Sierra Madre** 1948   126 mins (cert PG)
Classic moral drama about three gold prospectors – *Humphrey
Bogart*, *Walter Huston* and *Tim Holt* – greedily fighting it out
down Mexico way.

★★ **The Trial** 1993   120 mins (cert 12)
Lengthy, all-too-faithful version of Kafka's surreal novel. *Kyle
MacLachlan* is the man arrested for reasons he can never
discover.

★★★★ **Truly, Madly, Deeply** 1991   106 mins (cert PG)
Alternately touching and hilarious tale of coming to terms with
grief. *Juliet Stevenson* is the woman trying to accept the death of
her partner, *Alan Rickman*.

★★★ **Turtle Diary** 1985   96 mins (cert PG)
Gently amusing fable of repressed couple, *Ben Kingsley* and
Glenda Jackson, brought together by desire to free giant turtles
from the zoo.

★★★★ **Twelve Angry Men** 1957   95 mins (cert U)
Terrific court-room drama focusing on the deliberations of a
murder case jury. Cast headed by *Henry Fonda*. Brilliant
directorial debut by Sidney Lumet.

★★★ **The Ugly American** 1962   120 mins (cert U)
Far from ugly *Marlon Brando* plays Ambassador – to Communist
Asian country – whose mistakes threaten political and personal
disaster.

★★★ **The Unbearable Lightness of Being** 1988   171 mins (cert 18)
Intelligent, absorbing character study, adapted from Milan
Kundera's novel, of a doctor, *Daniel Day-Lewis*, reluctantly
involved in political and sexual conflict.

★★★★ **Under Fire** 1983   128 mins (cert 15)
Nick Nolte and *Gene Hackman* as journalists on the front line of
Nicaraguan rebellion in tense political thriller.

★★★ **Untamed Heart** 1993   102 mins (cert 15)
Busboy *Christian Slater* falls in love with waitress *Marisa Tomei*,
but he has a weak heart. Not so this movie. Touching, in parts
funny – thanks to *Rosie Perez* – and heart in the right place.

★★ **Valmont** 1989   137 mins (cert 15)
Milos Forman's version of Chodelos de Laclos' story of sex,
corruption and decadence in 18th-century France. Duffers in
comparison with 'Dangerous Liaisons'.

★★★ **The Verdict** 1982   128 mins (cert 15)
Disillusioned, dead-beat lawyer, *Paul Newman*, gets his act
together to fight case of medical negligence. Splendidly directed
by Sidney Lumet.

★★★ **Vincent and Theo** 1990   140 mins (cert 15)
Robert Altman's fine study of the relationship between Vincent
Van Gogh and his brother. A convincing performance by *Tim
Roth* as Vincent.

★★ **Vital Signs** 1990   103 mins (cert 15)
Pleasant enough attempt to do a sort of 'Doctor in the House'
in contemporary America. Nice young cast boosted by the likes
of *Jimmy Smits* and *William Devane*.

★★★ **Wall Street** 1987   124 mins (cert 15)
Oliver Stone's bleak indictment of greed and corruption among
stock brokers. *Michael Douglas* and *Charlie Sheen* star.

★ **War Party** 1989   96 mins (cert 18)
History repeats itself when abused, disgruntled, contemporary
Red Indians go to war with the Paleface.

★★★ **The Waterdance** 1992   107 mins (cert 15)
An entrancing story about a paraplegic hospital ward and the
courage and humour displayed therein. *Eric Stoltz* and *Wesley
Snipes* are two of the crippled inmates. A performance-led
drama.

★★ **Waterland** 1992   95 mins (cert 15)
Evocative but slow tale of teacher, *Jeremy Irons*, recounting his
childhood in the fens during WWII to his young American
students.

★★★ **What's Love Got To Do With It?** 1993   118 mins (cert 18)
Well-made biography of Tina Turner – played by *Angela Bassett*,
though great lady herself provides the soundtrack. *Larry
Fishburne* as the evil ex-husband, Ike.

★★★ **When the Whales Came** 1989   100 mins (cert U)
Deaf loner *Paul Scofield* and two young children try to save a
beached whale from hungry islanders. Unusual, offbeat story.

★★★ **Where Angels Fear to Tread** 1990   113 mins (cert PG)
This is not quite as pretty as Merchant Ivory usually manage
with E M Forster adaptations. Nicely acted though by *Helena
Bonham Carter*, *Judy Davis* and *Rupert Graves*.

★★ **Where No Vultures Fly** 1951   107 mins (cert U)
British docudrama relating conception of Mount Kilimanjaro
Game Reserve in Kenya. *Anthony Steele* and *Dinah Sheridan* star.

★★ **White Fang** 1991   108 mins (cert PG)
Ethan Hawke prospecting for gold in the Klondike finds friends:
orphan wolf cub and *Klaus Maria Brandauer*.

★★★ **White Hunter, Black Heart** 1990   112 mins (cert PG)
Clint Eastwood as a director – a thinly-disguised John Huston –
more obsessed with shooting an elephant than his movie.
(Incidentally, the movie was 'The African Queen'.)

★★ **White Mischief** 1988   106 mins (cert 18)
Lusty sex and murder saga of expatriate community in Kenya
with *Greta Scacchi*, *Charles Dance* and *Joss Ackland*.

★★★ **White Palace** 1990   105 mins (cert 18)
Sexy drama with *James Spader* as a yuppie widower falling for older, down-trodden waitress, *Susan Sarandon*.

. . . .

★★★★ **Who's Afraid of Virginia Woolf?** 1966   131 mins (cert 18)
Elizabeth Taylor and *Richard Burton*, a perfect partnership, as academic couple in ferocious marital relationship.

. . . .

★★ **Whose Life Is It Anyway?** 1981   118 mins (cert 15)
Richard Dreyfuss is fine as an artist, paralysed in an accident, fighting for his right to die but the film is too obviously stage-based.

. . . .

★★★ **Wild at Heart** 1990   127 mins (cert 18)
. . . and weird on top. Ferocious, funny and kinky David Lynch tale of *Nicolas Cage* and *Laura Dern* as a bizarre couple on the run.

. . . .

★★★★ **The Winslow Boy** 1950   117 mins (cert U)
Superb drama casts *Robert Donat* as barrister employed to clear name of *Cedric Hardwicke*'s son, no matter the cost to self or family.

. . . .

★★★ **Women in Love** 1970   127 mins (cert 18)
Ken Russell's raunchy version of D H Lawrence's tale of love and sex. Stars *Glenda Jackson*, *Alan Bates* and *Oliver Reed*. Famous (notorious?) nude, male wrestling scene.

. . . .

★★★ **A World Apart** 1988   110 mins (cert PG)
Highly charged drama set in South Africa. *Barbara Hershey*'s bitter struggle against apartheid as seen through the eyes of her daughter, *Jodhi May*.

. . . .

★ **Wuthering Heights** 1992   106 mins (cert U)
Oh dear. Do read the book. Dull adaptation of one of the great books. *Ralph Fiennes* and *Juliette Binoche* woefully miscast as Heathcliffe and Cathy.

. . . .

★★★ **Yanks** 1979   139 mins (cert 15)
Engaging story of Americans billeted in small-town England during WWII and the lives and loves they leave behind. *Richard Gere* leads.

★★★ **The Year of Living Dangerously** 1983   115 mins (cert PG)
Fine performances projected *Mel Gibson* and *Sigourney Weaver* to
stardom as a couple investigating political crisis in Indonesia.
Linda Hunt won Oscar as Gibson's (male) side-kick.

★★★ **Zorba the Greek** 1964   146 mins (cert PG)
Lusty drama set in small village on Crete where colourful
native, *Anthony Quinn*, teaches Englishman *Alan Bates* how to get
the most out of life.

FAMILY

★★ **The Addams Family** 1991   99 mins (cert PG)
Ghoulish comic strip family brought to life Hollywood-style by
Anjelica Huston, *Raul Julia* and *Christopher Lloyd* as Uncle Fester –
who may or may not be an impostor.

★★★ **Addams Family Values** 1993   96 mins (cert PG)
Better than original with a stronger story and more effective
jokes – every one a winner. *Christina Ricci* as Wednesday
outshines the adult cast.

★★★★ **Aladdin** 1993   90 mins (cert U)
Disney's 31st animated feature film is the highest grossing
cartoon ever, based on the fable of the Arabian Nights. *Robin
Williams* is superb as the voice of the hip and happening genie.

★★ **All Dogs Go to Heaven** 1989   84 mins (cert U)
Disney-style animation made in Ireland. *Burt Reynolds* provides
voice of the canine hero. So-so family fun.

★ **All I Want for Christmas** 1991   90 mins (cert U)
Sentimental tale centring on children's scheme to reunite
parents. Slushy but seasonal.

★★★ **An American Tail** 1986   81 mins (cert U)
Steven Spielberg's animated fantasy of Russian mouse family
emigrating to an America whose streets, they hope, are paved
with cheese.

★★ **An American Tail II: Fievel Goes West** 1991   74 mins (cert U)
Further, though rather weaker, adventures of the Mouskewitz
family.

★★ **Anne of Green Gables** 1985   79 mins (cert U)
Spirited orphan, *Megan Follows*, wins love of lonely old couple in
remake of better 1934 movie.

★★ **Arachnophobia** 1990   110 mins (cert PG)
Slick, Spielberg-produced, comic thriller about a small town
overrun by killer spiders. Less scary than you might expect.

★★★ **Around the World in 80 Days** 1965   178 mins (cert U)
David Niven as the intrepid Phileas Fogg who wagers he can travel the globe in less than three months. A glittering cast of guest stars adds interest and sparkle.

★★★★ **Bambi** 1942   69 mins (cert U)
Disney's telling of the little fawn growing up in the forest still has them weeping in the aisles and crying with joy at the end. Timeless classic.

★★ **The Bear** 1989   93 mins (cert PG)
Patronisingly anthropomorphic tale of an ursine family, but at the same time a beautifully filmed story of a cub and its fight for survival.

★★★★ **Beauty and the Beast** 1992   84 mins (cert U)
First animated feature ever nominated for Best Film Oscar – deservedly so. The Disney studio shows it can still produce excellent fairytale features better than anyone else.

★★★ **Beethoven** 1991   87 mins (cert U)
A St Bernard dog causes chaos for canine-hater *Charles Grodin* and family, and rounds up the bad guys. Grodin provides a sharp edge to cut the sugar.

★★★ **Big** 1988   105 mins (cert PG)
Tom Hanks gives spirited performance as a twelve-year-old boy in an adult body and an adult world. The best of a bunch of life-swap movies that came out around that time – heaven knows why.

★★ **Bill and Ted's Bogus Journey** 1991   93 mins (cert PG)
The dudes travel through heaven and hell in an amusing sequel notable for jokes, special effects and *Bill Sadler*'s Grim Reaper.

★★★ **Bill and Ted's Excellent Adventure** 1989   89 mins (cert PG)
Keanu Reeves and *Alex Winter* as the cool but dim dudes given a history lesson via a time-machine phone box, so that, one day, they might save the world. Lively fun.

★★★ **Born Free** 1966   95 mins (cert U)
Visually stunning biopic of Joy Adamson raising orphaned lion in Kenya. *Virginia McKenna* and *Bill Travers* lead.

★★ **Buffy the Vampire Slayer** 1991   94 mins (cert 12)
Valley girl *Kirsty Swanson* and loner *Luke Perry* clean up their
neighbourhood, overrun by vampires led by *Rutger Hauer*.
Highschool comic horror.

★★★ **Bugsy Malone** 1976   93 mins (cert U)
Alan Parker directs cast of children in 1920s gangster musical.
Enjoyable romp. Twelve-year-old *Jodie Foster* stars.

★★ **Captain America** 1990   97 mins (cert PG)
Comic book hero, *Matt Salinger*, patriotically sporting the stars
and stripes, saves the US president from terrorists. Predictable.

★★ **Champions** 1992   104 mins (cert PG)
Emilio Estevez as hot-shot lawyer sentenced to community
service training no-hope young ice hockey team. Lessons
learned all round, not least by Estevez. (Called 'The Mighty
Ducks' in USA.)

★★ **A Christmas Carol** 1984   100 mins (cert U)
Prettily restaged version of Dickens' tale. *George C Scott* as
Scrooge is better than the rest of it.

★★★ **Cocoon** 1985   117 mins (cert PG)
Florida oldies find the fountain of youth, courtesy of visiting
aliens, in warm, sentimental fable.

★★ **Cocoon: The Return** 1988   110 mins (cert PG)
Predictable sequel with the old folk returning to Earth for a
visit. Great cast, shame about the script.

★ **Cool World** 1992   102 mins (cert 12)
Cartoon combining live and animated action about a cartoonist,
Gabriel Byrne, who enters the fantasy world he's created but is
followed out by his sexy heroine, *Kim Basinger*. Dire script.

★★ **Cop and a Half** 1993   93 mins (cert PG)
Cop and kid makes an amusing variation on buddy, buddy
theme thanks to straight playing by *Burt Reynolds* and the appeal
of young *Norman D Golden III* as witness and solver of crime.

★★★★ **Crocodile Dundee** 1986   98 mins (cert 15)
Surprisingly but deservedly successful yarn about outback
woodsman, *Paul Hogan*, uprooted to Manhattan. Great fun.

★★ **Crocodile Dundee II** 1988   111 mins (cert PG)
More violence, fewer jokes, as *Paul Hogan* leaves Manhattan and returns to Oz to trap drug dealers.

★ **Curly Sue** 1991   102 mins (cert PG)
Slushy John Hughes comedy. Precocious little girl gets a mother for Christmas but who cares?

★★★ **The Dark Crystal** 1983   93 mins (cert PG)
Muppets creator Jim Henson's dark, superbly animated fable of good and evil.

★★★★ **David Copperfield** 1935   133 mins (cert U)
MGM's version of Dickens' masterpiece. *W C Fields* hilariously playing a juggling Mr McCawber heads terrific cast.

★★ **Dennis** 1993   94 mins (cert PG)
Precocious child gives *Walter Matthau* a hard time. NOT to be confused with Dennis the Menace.

★★★ **Dick Tracy** 1990   103 mins (cert PG)
Warren Beatty's visually splendid version of gang-busting comic book hero. *Madonna* co-stars, but *Al Pacino* steals the show.

★★★ **Doc Hollywood** 1991   104 mins (cert 12)
Enchanting comic fairytale of budding plastic surgeon, *Michael J Fox*, lured from fame and fortune in city job by charm of small-town life.

★★★★ **Dumbo** 1941   90 mins (cert U)
Wealth of characters makes Disney's animation of a flying elephant always worth watching.

★★★★ **Edward Scissorhands** 1990   105 mins (cert PG)
Johnny Depp as the man-made boy with blades for hands exposed to 1950s small-town America. Lovely fantasy marred by harsh ending.

★★★ **Fantasia** 1940   135 mins (cert U)
Walt Disney's stunning, innovative blend of animation and classical music. A minor work of art.

★★★ **Ferngully: The Last Rain Forest** 1993   76 mins (cert U)
Animated tale of forest folk fighting fiendish tree fellers. Strong on humour and ecology with voices supplied by *Robin Williams*, *Christian Slater* and *Samantha Mathis*.

★★★★★ **Field of Dreams** 1989   106 mins (cert PG)
Perfectly life-enhancing fantasy of farmer, *Kevin Costner*, told by a disembodied voice to build a baseball pitch among his crops so that late, great players may return. Magical.

★★ **Freddie as F.R.O.7.** 1991   91 mins (cert U)
Prince turned into frog secret agent on trail of missing London landmarks. Voiced by *Ben Kingsley*, *Jenny Agutter*, *Brian Blessed* and *Nigel Hawthorne*.

★★★★ **The Frog Prince** 1985   90 mins (cert 15)
Delightful modern-day fairytale set against beautiful Parisian backdrop.

★★★★ **Genevieve** 1953   86 mins (cert U)
Delightful British romp about the rivalry between classic car owners *Kenneth Moore* and *John Gregson* during London to Brighton race and after.

★ **The Golden Child** 1986   93 mins (cert PG)
Profoundly silly comedy/thriller in which *Eddie Murphy*'s lazy performance first revealed his feet of clay.

★★★ **The Golden Voyage of Sinbad** 1974   105 mins (cert U)
Colourful adaptation of Arabian Nights adventure. Special effects better than the acting.

★★★★★ **Great Expectations** 1946   100 mins (cert PG)
David Lean pays admirable homage to Dickens' classic story. *John Mills* as Pip, *Alec Guinness* as Herbert Pocket.

★★★ **The Great Mouse Detective** 1986   80 mins (cert U)
Engaging Disney animated cartoon with Sherlock Holmes as a mouse solving the mysterious disappearance of a toymaker.

★★★ **Gremlins** 1984   111 mins (cert 15)
Cute little creatures turn vicious if fed after midnight in adult children's story from the Spielberg stable.

★★ **Gremlins 2: The New Batch** 1990   107 mins (cert 12)
Special effects are an improvement on original but the story's
weaker.

★★★★ **Hobson's Choice** 1953   107 mins (cert U)
Stirring yet comic performance from *Charles Laughton* as a
conservative father opposed to his daughter's wedding. David
Lean directed.

★★ **Hocus Pocus** 1993   97 mins (cert PG)
Bette Midler, *Sarah Jessica Parker* and *Kathy Nijimy* play three
witches who are reawakened after 300 years. They are offered
immortality if they can eat the town's children before dawn but
are hampered by the fact that it's Halloween.

★★★ **Home Alone** 1990   103 mins (cert PG)
Eight-year-old *Macaulay Culkin*, mistakenly left at home alone
for Christmas, fights off burglars and discovers the value of
family life. Overly sentimental but amusing.

★★ **Home Alone 2: Lost in New York** 1992   120 mins (cert PG)
Macaulay Culkin abandoned by his family at Christmas again.
(Has he ever heard of Childline?) This year he's in the Big
Apple and again facing hapless burglars *Joe Pesci* and *Daniel
Stern*. The violence is taken too far and the humour and charm
of the original are quite lost.

★ **Homeward Bound: The Incredible Journey** 1993   85 mins (cert U)
Awful remake of the Disney original. The two dogs and a cat
crossing dangerous terrain to reach their human family are
obnoxious due to the voice-overs from *Michael J Fox*, *Don Ameche*
and *Sally Field*.

★ **Honey, I Blew Up the Kid** 1992   89 mins (cert U)
Dim sequel. *Rick Moranis* still tinkering with inventions that do
strange things to his kids. This time he turns the new baby into
a 100-foot, nappy nightmare.

★★★ **Honey, I Shrunk the Kids** 1989   93 mins (cert U)
Scientist, *Rick Moranis*, mistakenly shrinks his and neighbour's
children to microscopic size. Family fun as kids fight for
survival.

★★ **Hook** 1992   144 mins (cert U)

Lavish but bastardized story of Peter Pan. *Robin Williams* as 'Pan the Man' grown up and having forgotten about Never, Never Land and the lost boys. *Dustin Hoffman* is the dastardly Captain Hook luring him back by snatching his children. Hard to believe Steven Spielberg was responsible for ruining such a great story.

★ **Howard the Duck** 1986   111 mins (cert PG)

George Lucas' mega-flop – a dreary, unlovable animated cartoon popularly known as 'Howard the Turkey'.

★★★★ **It's a Wonderful Life** 1946   129 mins (cert U)

And a wonderful film. A Frank Capra classic in which *James Stewart*, the would-be suicide, is shown by his guardian angel what life would be like without him. Just about as joyful as they come.

★★★ **Jason and the Argonauts** 1963   104 mins (cert U)

Ray Harryhausen's special effects dominate in this legendary adventure of search for the Golden Fleece. Great stuff.

★★★★ **The Jungle Book** 1967   78 mins (cert U)

Disney never bettered musically. Brilliant swinging numbers make this a true joy, though animated version bears little resemblance to Kipling's novel.

★★★★ **Jurassic Park** 1993   132 mins (cert PG)

Highest grossing film ever. *Richard Attenborough* in charge of a dinosaur park; *Jeff Goldblum*, *Laura Dern*, et al, the unlucky visitors. Marvellous effects and direction (by Steven Spielberg) when all hell breaks loose.

★★ **Kidnapped** 1971   107 mins (cert U)

Stevenson's cracking and often filmed adventure story is done justice by solid British cast headed by *Michael Caine*.

★★★ **Labyrinth** 1986   101 mins (cert U)

Pleasing Jim Henson fantasy in which teenager *Jennifer Connolly* must find her way through a menacing maze to save her little brother, kidnapped by goblins.

★★★★ **Lady and the Tramp** 1955   75 mins (cert U)

Timeless Disney delight. Animated adventures of well-bred spaniel and her raffish mongrel boyfriend.

★★ **Ladyhawke** 1985   124 mins (cert PG)
Lavish fantasy based on 700-year-old legend of lovers, *Michelle Pfeiffer* and *Rutger Hauer*, separated by a curse which turns her into a hawk by day. Should have been better.

⋯⋯⋯⋯⋯⋯⋯⋯⋯⋯⋯⋯⋯⋯⋯⋯⋯⋯⋯⋯⋯⋯⋯⋯⋯⋯⋯⋯⋯⋯⋯⋯⋯⋯⋯⋯⋯

★ **Lionheart** 1987   99 mins (cert PG)
A band of youngsters led by *Eric Stoltz* search for missing King Richard and defend his throne.

⋯⋯⋯⋯⋯⋯⋯⋯⋯⋯⋯⋯⋯⋯⋯⋯⋯⋯⋯⋯⋯⋯⋯⋯⋯⋯⋯⋯⋯⋯⋯⋯⋯⋯⋯⋯⋯

★★ **The Little Mermaid** 1989   82 mins (cert U)
Disney's delightful – though much softened – adaptation of Hans Christian Anderson fairytale.

⋯⋯⋯⋯⋯⋯⋯⋯⋯⋯⋯⋯⋯⋯⋯⋯⋯⋯⋯⋯⋯⋯⋯⋯⋯⋯⋯⋯⋯⋯⋯⋯⋯⋯⋯⋯⋯

★★★ **The Little Princess** 1939   91 mins (cert U)
Shirley Temple (in colour for the first time) at her cutest as poor little rich girl cruelly mistreated at boarding school.

⋯⋯⋯⋯⋯⋯⋯⋯⋯⋯⋯⋯⋯⋯⋯⋯⋯⋯⋯⋯⋯⋯⋯⋯⋯⋯⋯⋯⋯⋯⋯⋯⋯⋯⋯⋯⋯

★★★★ **Local Hero** 1983   111 mins (cert PG)
Bill Forsyth's delightful examination of effect on Scottish coastal village when American tycoon wants to buy it for oil refinery.

⋯⋯⋯⋯⋯⋯⋯⋯⋯⋯⋯⋯⋯⋯⋯⋯⋯⋯⋯⋯⋯⋯⋯⋯⋯⋯⋯⋯⋯⋯⋯⋯⋯⋯⋯⋯⋯

★★★ **The Love Bug** 1969   107 mins (cert U)
Herbie's first and best outing as the VW Beetle with a mind of its own.

⋯⋯⋯⋯⋯⋯⋯⋯⋯⋯⋯⋯⋯⋯⋯⋯⋯⋯⋯⋯⋯⋯⋯⋯⋯⋯⋯⋯⋯⋯⋯⋯⋯⋯⋯⋯⋯

★★ **Mary Poppins** 1964   140 mins (cert U)
Disney's musical version of the no-nonsense, magical nanny. *Julie Andrews* somewhat miscast, *Dick Van Dyke* much more so as her improbable Cockney beau.

⋯⋯⋯⋯⋯⋯⋯⋯⋯⋯⋯⋯⋯⋯⋯⋯⋯⋯⋯⋯⋯⋯⋯⋯⋯⋯⋯⋯⋯⋯⋯⋯⋯⋯⋯⋯⋯

★ **Meet the Applegates** 1991   90 mins (cert 15)
Insects in human guise plot to end the world in weak but inoffensive fable.

⋯⋯⋯⋯⋯⋯⋯⋯⋯⋯⋯⋯⋯⋯⋯⋯⋯⋯⋯⋯⋯⋯⋯⋯⋯⋯⋯⋯⋯⋯⋯⋯⋯⋯⋯⋯⋯

★★★ **Miracle on 34th Street** 1947   92 mins (cert U)
Enchanting fantasy of department store Santa put on trial to prove he really is Father Christmas. With *Maureen O'Hara* and *Edmund Gwenn*.

⋯⋯⋯⋯⋯⋯⋯⋯⋯⋯⋯⋯⋯⋯⋯⋯⋯⋯⋯⋯⋯⋯⋯⋯⋯⋯⋯⋯⋯⋯⋯⋯⋯⋯⋯⋯⋯

★★★★ **Moonstruck** 1987   102 mins (cert PG)
Enchanting romantic comedy set in Little Italy where *Cher* falls in love with fiancé's brother, *Nicolas Cage*. Mistake to miss this. It's life enhancing.

★★ **Mr Nanny** 1993   84 mins (cert PG)
Wrestler *Hulk Hogan* hired as nanny to protect the spoilt kids of
threatened scientist *Austin Pendleton*. Pretty brutal in parts,
amusing in others.

★ **Mr Destiny** 1990   105 mins (cert PG)
Mild fantasy which wastes a good cast – *James Belushi*, *Linda
Hamilton*, *Michael Caine* – about an oddball who returns to high
school to replay an old baseball game.

★★ **The Muppet Christmas Carol** 1992   85 mins (cert U)
Kermit as Tom Cratchitt, Miss Piggy in dream role as his wife
and *Michael Caine* as Scrooge. Nice one for all Muppet fans.

★ **My Girl** 1991   102 mins (cert PG)
Sentimental rites-of-passage stuff with *Dan Aykroyd*, *Macaulay
Culkin* (getting his first screen kiss – Gosh!) and a woefully
wasted *Jamie Lee Curtis*.

★★ **My Grandad's a Vampire** 1992   95 mins (cert U)
Jolly children's romp. Is grandad really a vampire? Kid's should
enjoy finding out – and they won't be too scared.

★★★ **National Velvet** 1944   125 mins (cert U)
Well-loved family movie. *Elizabeth Taylor* determined to ride her
horse to victory in the Grand National.

★★★ **The Neverending Story** 1984   94 mins (cert U)
Children's adventure about a small boy entering the magical
land in his story book. Good effects; not a bad yarn.

★★ **The Neverending Story 2** 1990   90 mins (cert U)
Plot's a little weak but the effects still impress in a further
adventure set in Fantasia.

★★ **The News Boys** 1992   121 mins (cert PG)
Ineffectual musical account of the newspaper boys' strike in
turn-of-the-century USA. Don't expect an 'Oliver!' here.

★ **Nukie** 1992   87 mins (cert U)
Two cute aliens separated on Earth are reunited by African
children.

★★ **Once Upon a Forest** 1993   68 mins (cert U)
Animated tale of forest polluted by noxious gases and the subsequent attempts of a mouse, hedgehog and mole to save the day. *Michael Crawford* sings, but don't let that put you off.

★★ **On Christmas Eve** 1993   25 mins (cert U)
A magical animated Christmas story of a little girl who has written to Father Christmas.

★★★ **Peter Pan** 1953   76 mins (cert U)
Disney animated feature of the classic J M Barrie story of the boy who never grows up.

★★ **Prancer** 1989   102 mins (cert U)
Children's fable of unhappy little girl who finds Santa's missing reindeer.

★★ **The Princess and the Goblin** 1993   98 mins (cert U)
Animated tale of princess who gets lost in forest, runs into goblins and is saved by a handsome miner's son. Voices by *Rik Mayall*, *Joss Ackland*, *Roy Kinnear*, *Claire Bloom* and *Molly Sugden*.

★★★ **The Princess Bride** 1987   98 mins (cert PG)
Enchanting fairytale adventure in which abducted princess, *Robin Wright*, must be rescued by dashing hero, *Cary Elwes*.

★★★★ **The Railway Children** 1972   108 mins (cert U)
Three children adapt to new life in the country when father's imprisoned on spying charge. Little gem of a picture.

★★ **The Rescuers** 1977   75 mins (cert U)
Animated adventure from the Disney studios involving the engaging exploits of trouble-shooting mice.

★★ **The Rescuers Down Under** 1990   77 mins (cert U)
More of the same. International Rescue Aid dispatches our two brave mice to save an Australian boy deep in trouble.

★★ **Rock-a-Doodle** 1990   74 mins (cert U)
Farmyard problems in this animated feature film when the rooster leaves for the city. Good songs, nice story.

★★★★ **The Secret Garden** 1993   101 mins (cert U)
A spellbinding version of the children's story of an orphan girl
sent to stay with her grieving uncle and crippled cousin. *Maggie
Smith* is the haunting housekeeper.

★★★★★ **The Thief of Baghdad** 1940   109 mins (cert U)
A magical film – the best Arabian Nights fantasy of them all.
John Justin as the prince, *Sabu* as the thief and *Conrad Veidt*
magnificent as the Vizier.

★★★ **Watership Down** 1978   92 mins (cert U)
Animated feature adaptation of Richard Adams' bestseller.
A family of rabbits face danger and death as they search for
a new home. A bit violent for the very young.

★★★★ **Who Framed Roger Rabbit?** 1988   103 mins (cert PG)
Outstanding animation combined with live action marks comic
caper of detective, *Bob Hoskins*, out to clear the name of the
wrongly accused rabbit.

★★★ **Willow** 1988   126 mins (cert PG)
Fantasy adventure of a dwarf guarding a baby saviour with the
help of *Val Kilmer* and *Joanne Whalley-Kilmer*.

★★★ **The Wind in the Willows** 1983   55 mins (cert U)
Beautiful adaptation of the great children's book. Voices are
provided by *David Jason*, *Michael Hordern*, *Peter Sallis* and *Ian
Carmichael*.

★★★ **The Witches** 1990   92 mins (cert PG)
At a British hotel, a small boy and his granny find themselves in
the middle of a witches' convention headed by *Anjelica Huston*.

★★★★★ **The Wizard of Oz** 1939   101 mins (cert U)
Shirley Temple was initial choice for Dorothy but, mercifully,
Judy Garland stepped into the ruby slippers for this enchanting,
fantasy musical.

★★ **The Wolves of Willoughby Chase** 1989   93 mins (cert PG)
Two young children left to the wicked wiles of *Mel Smith* and
Stephanie Beecham are sent to a dark Dickensian orphanage.

FOREIGN

★★★ **A Bout de Souffle** 1959   90 mins   (cert 18)
Jean-Luc Godard's stylish movie of Parisian car thief, *Jean Paul Belmondo*, on the run with his American girlfriend, *Jean Seberg*, for killing a policeman.

★★ **L'Accompagnatrice** 1993   111 mins   (cert PG)
Set in occupied France and wartime London. Singer *Elena Safonova*'s accompanist acts as go-between for her and resistance lover. Nice idea but rather flat and unconvincing.

★★★ **Agantu** 1992   120 mins   (cert U)
The last film by Indian director Satyajit Ray, about a family thrown into disarray after receiving a letter from a long lost uncle.

★★ **The Anchoress** 1993   108 mins   (cert 12)
Heavy-handed 14th-century tale wherein *Natalie Morse* – who is obsessed with the Virgin Mary – is proclaimed a holy anchoress and walled up in the church. Looks pretty, lacks substance and coherence.

★★★ **The Assault** 1986   155 mins   (cert PG)
Thought-provoking drama of Dutch survivor of WWII tracing events that led to the slaughter of his family. Won best foreign film Oscar.

★★★★ **Au Revoir les Enfants** 1987   107 mins   (cert PG)
Classy, affecting film from Louis Malle which tells of a group of Jewish children at boarding school in occupied France during WWII.

★★★★ **Babette's Feast** 1987   102 mins   (cert U)
Delightful adaptation of Isak Dinesen's tale of a French refugee, *Stephane Audran*, who cooks the world's greatest meal for two Danish sisters who have befriended her.

★★★ **La Balance** 1982   102 mins   (cert 18)
Violent, thrilling French crime story. Prostitute and petty criminal pressed to give evidence against crime boss. *Nathalie Baye* as the hooker.

★★★★★ **The Battleship Ptomekin** 1925   86 mins (cert U)
Eisenstein's great silent movie about the crew of a Russian
battleship during the mutiny at Odessa. One of the most
influential films ever made.

★★ **Betty Blue** 1986   121 mins (cert 18)
Visually impressive French film of mad waitress and odd-job
man travelling around country. Noted for opening sex scenes.
Not as good as its cult following would suggest.

★★★ **La Cage aux Folles** 1978   91 mins (cert 15)
Very funny French comedy. Two gay lovers pose as straights
when the son of one of them wants to get married. (Followed
by two sequels, the first of which is pretty good but forget the
other.)

★★★ **Cinema Paradiso** 1988   124 mins (cert PG)
Italian gem about young boy's love of the cinema. Steeped in
charm, especially the early section with *Philippe Noiret* and
young *Salvatore Cascio*. (Re-released, an hour longer, in 1993.
Longer is not necessarily better.)

★★★★ **Claire's Knee** 1971   106 mins (cert 12)
One of Eric Rohmer's fascinating moral tales. Engaged young
man becomes obsessed with knee of girl he doesn't even like.

★★★★ **Un Coeur en Hiver** 1992   105 mins (cert 12)
Emmanuelle Beart stars in an adult, sophisticated love triangle
with *Daniel Autueil* and *Andre Dussollier*. The kind of film only the
French know how to make.

★★★ **Cop au Vin** 1984   109 mins (cert 15)
Claude Chabrol's engaging 'policier' in which a cop investigates
the murder of a thug by a young boy.

★★★ **Cup Final** 1992   107 mins (cert 15)
Israeli soldier and his Palestinian captors in Lebanon find they
have more in common than just a love of football and a desire
to watch the 1982 World Cup Final. Lovely slant on war and
human nature.

★★★★ **Cyrano de Bergerac** 1990   135 mins (cert U)
Outstanding adaptation of Rostand play with *Gerard Depardieu*
superb as the poet, swordsman and vicarious lover.

★★★★ **Danton** 1982   136 mins (cert PG)
Gerard Depardieu memorable in Andrzej Wajda's dramatic
reconstruction of the Reign of Terror in 18th-century Paris.

★★★ **Delicatessen** 1991   97 mins (cert 15)
Shocking, funny French tale that hovers between farce and
horror centred on cannibalistic inhabitants of apartment block.
You don't want to make friends with the butcher.

★★★ **Diva** 1982   117 mins (cert 15)
Stylish high-tech melodrama about French music lover who is
unwittingly involved with underworld after illicitly taping a
diva's concert.

★★★★ **La Dolce Vita** 1960   173 mins (cert 18)
Fellini's surreal Italian drama of reporter *Marcello Mastroianni*'s
adventures in decadent Roman society. Bit dated now but one
of the seminal films of its time.

★★★ **8½** 1963   138 mins (cert 15)
Portrait of a film director, *Marcello Mastroianni*, on the verge of a
nervous breakdown and fantasizing about his life. Viewed by
many as Fellini's masterpiece.

★★★★ **Les Enfants du Paradis** 1945   195 mins (cert PG)
Marcel Carne's marvellous theatrical extravaganza of 1840s
Paris made during WWII. Poetic romance superbly conceived,
superbly played.

★★ **Everybody's Fine** 1990   112 mins (cert PG)
The darker side of nostalgia in Italian tale of old man, *Marcello
Mastroianni*, on visit to family finding everybody's not as fine as
he thought.

★★★ **Fanny and Alexander** 1983   197 mins (cert 15)
Sumptuous family saga by Ingmar Bergman (his last film as a
director) which deals with the fortunes of two children in turn-
of-the-century Sweden. (The TV version runs for 420 minutes.)

★★★★ **Farewell, My Concubine** 1993   128 mins (cert 15)
Story of the rise and fall of two opera stars set against the
background of changing China from 1920s to 1970s. A lavish
costume drama well worth a look.

★★★ **La Fille de L'Air** 1993   106 mins (cert 15)
Beatrice Dalle risks family to spring her husband from jail. Based on a true story but hard to believe it's based on fact.

....

★★★ **Fitzcarraldo** 1982   158 mins (cert PG)
Klaus Kinski excels in German film of a crazy Irishman dragging a steamship over a hill to build an opera house in turn-of-the-century Peru.

....

★★ **Hard Boiled** 1993   126 mins (cert 18)
Exceptionally violent and unpleasant story of Hong Kong cops and killers battling to bust smuggling ring. John Woo directs.

....

★★★ **High Heels** 1991   115 mins (cert 18)
Spanish director Pedro Almodovar's spicy tale of a mother and daughter's relationship helped and hindered by the death of *Victoria Abril*'s husband – her mother's one-time lover.

....

★★★ **Hiroshima, Mon Amour** 1960   91 mins (cert 18)
Alain Resnais' unusual, thoughtful story about love affair of French actress and Japanese architect in post-war Hiroshima.

....

★★ **Indochine** 1992   120 mins (cert 12)
Catherine Deneuve looks as good as ever in an epic tale set in SE Asia during the French occupation, but the story ambles nowhere in the end.

....

★★ **IP5** 1993   98 mins (cert 15)
Yves Montand's final performance as an elderly man searching for his lost love in the company of a graffiti artist and a Paris rapper. Bizarre and inconclusive.

....

★★ **Jamon Jamon** 1993   120 mins (cert 18)
Bizarre Spanish love tangle. Girl loves boy who's sleeping with her mother. Girl sleeps with boy's father. Boy's mother hires another boy to seduce girl and sleeps with him herself. All ends with brains being bashed out by legs of ham. Everyday plot really . . .

....

★★★★ **Jean de Florette** 1986   122 mins (cert PG)
Beautifully shot, perfectly acted French country soap. *Gerard Depardieu* is the farmer duped by conniving neighbour, *Yves Montand*.

★★★ **Jesus of Montreal** 1989   120 mins (cert 18)
Denis Arcaud's morality play in which actor, *Lothaire Bluteau*, portraying Jesus is mistaken for the real thing.

....

★★★★ **Kagemusha** 1980   181 mins (cert PG)
16th-century Japanese thief poses as dead warlord to safeguard the throne in Kurosawa's marvellous epic.

....

★★★ **The Legend of the Holy Drinker** 1988   120 mins (cert PG)
Affecting adaptation of Joseph Roth novella with *Rutger Hauer* as a Parisian tramp offered money by a stranger if he will give it back to a chapel when he can.

....

★ **Léolo** 1993   107 mins (cert 18)
Italian boy believes he was conceived by a tomato. Preferable to his family whose madness is slowly revealed in this strange drama.

....

★ **The Lie** 1993   89 mins (cert 15)
Better remove all sharp objects before watching this – it's a phenomenally depressing French morality play. *Nathalie Baye* discovers that not only is she pregnant, she also has AIDS and sets about discovering what her husband's been up to.

....

★★★ **Like Water for Chocolate** 1993   114 mins (cert 15)
Intriguing feast of a movie about love, sex, food and families, starting in Mexico at the turn of the century. Quite bizarre but hypnotic.

....

★★ **Madame Bovary** 1992   140 mins (cert PG)
Claude Chabrol's rather dull version of Flaubert's classic. *Isabelle Hubert* as the wayward Emma, seeking love and social status in 19th-century France.

....

★★★ **Man Bites Dog** 1992   96 mins (cert 18)
Hilarious, violent, pitch-black comedy about a documentary crew filming a serial killer at work. One scene is so brutal it will wipe the smile off your face, but drives the message home. Best Belgian film ever made.

....

★★★★ **Manon des Sources** 1986   114 mins (cert PG)
Equally impressive sequel to 'Jean de Florette' with Gerard Depardieu's daughter seeks revenge on *Yves Montand*.

★★ **Mediterraneo** 1993   86 mins (cert 15)
During WWII eight Italian soldiers are abandoned on a Greek island. Gradually they begin to enjoy a blissful idyll. Charming but insubstantial.

★★★★ **Mephisto** 1981   144 mins (cert 15)
Klaus Maria Brandauer as the actor whose ambition leads him to sell out to the Nazis. Riveting movie which shows that Brandauer, in German, is one of the best screen actors in the world.

★★★ **Monsieur Hire** 1989   82 mins (cert 15)
Peeping Tom falls in love with beautiful neighbour involved in murder. Taut, tense adaptation of Simenon story.

★★★★ **Monsieur Hulot's Holiday** 1953   86 mins (cert U)
Jacques Tati as accident prone bachelor causing chaos at the seaside in a lovely, virtually silent, comedy.

★★★★ **My Father's Glory** 1991   105 mins (cert U)
Marcel Pagnol's utterly charming account of his childhood in southern France during the early part of century.

★★★★ **My Life as a Dog** 1985   101 mins (cert PG)
Poignant Swedish comedy about mischievous boy sent to live with aunt and uncle. Many people chose this as the best film of the 1980s.

★★★ **My Mother's Castle** 1991   103 mins (cert 12)
Marcel Pagnol continues his reminiscences of French childhood in a companion piece to 'My Father's Glory'.

★★★★ **The Nasty Girl** 1990   108 mins (cert 15)
Fine blend of humour and drama in young woman's attempt to uncover her hometown's guilty, Nazi past.

★★★ **Olivier, Olivier** 1992   105 mins (cert 15)
Young boy disappears in rural France only to return years later. His family welcomes him back – but is he the real Olivier? An intriguing tale.

★★★ **The Ox** 1992   92 mins (cert 12)
Based on a true story and telling of the drastic effect of the theft of a cow on a Swedish village struck by famine during 19th-century crop failure. *Max von Sydow* heads a fine cast.

★★★★ **Pandora's Box** 1929   97 mins (cert 15)
Silent German masterpiece with a legendary performance by
Louise Brooks as the sexually provocative Lulu who ends up in the
hands of Jack the Ripper.

★★★ **Pelle the Conqueror** 1988   155 mins (cert 15)
Deeply moving Swedish drama about a widower, *Max von Sydow*,
and young son struggling to survive as immigrants in Denmark.

★★★ **Pixote** 1981   127 mins (cert 18)
Harrowing Brazilian exposé of plight of homeless children
driven to crime, drugs and prostitution on the streets of Rio.

★★★ **Playtime** 1967   152 mins (cert U)
Monsieur Hulot finds himself in a futuristic Paris in *Jacques
Tati*'s comedy delight.

★★★ **Les Quatre Cents Coups** 1959   94 mins (cert 15)
François Truffaut's innovative autobiographical account of a
young boy, *Jean-Pierre Léaud*, who, neglected by his parents,
turns to petty crime and is sent to reform school.

★★★ **The Quince Tree Sun** 1993   139 mins (cert U)
Some may find watching grass grow more entertaining than
this film about a painter painting a tree. And that's all he does.
Yet it's strangely hypnotic and rather fascinating.

★★★★ **Ran** 1985   161 mins (cert 15)
Stunning Japanese version of 'King Lear' by master movie-
maker Akira Kurosawa.

★★★ **Red Sorghum** 1987   92 mins (cert 15)
Evocative, moving story of a young Chinese couple in the 1920s
and 1930s. Rich in detail, visually spectacular.

★★★★★ **La Regle du Jeu** 1939   113 mins (cert 15)
Jean Renoir's tragi-comic masterpiece about love and intrigue
among houseguests at a weekend shooting party. A truly great
film.

★★★ **Le Retour de Martin Guerre** 1982   123 mins (cert 15)
16th-century French tale – based on fact – of a villager, *Gerard
Depardieu*, returning home a changed character. But is he really
Martin Guerre? Remade as 'Sommersby'.

★★★★ Romuald et Juliette 1989   107 mins (cert 12)
Warm but sharp romantic comedy with lovers *Daniel Auteuil* and *Firmine Richard* crossing barriers of class and colour.

....

★★★ La Ronde 1950   110 mins (cert 18)
Max Ophul's delicious French farce in which a chain of illicit love affairs comes full circle. Was thought dead saucy in its day.

....

★★ Savage Nights 1993   126 mins (cert 18)
Autobiographical story by Frenchman *Cyril Collard*, who died of AIDS just after completing the film, provides a frank look at his promiscuous bi-sexual lifestyle.

....

★ Schtonk 1992   111 mins (cert 15)
Dull German comedy inspired – if that's the word – by the forged Hitler diaries.

....

★★★★★ The Seven Samurai 1954   155 mins (cert 15)
Akira Kurosawa's masterpiece from which 'The Magnificent Seven' was taken. Must be on everyone's list of the ten best.

....

★★★★★ The Seventh Seal 1957   95 mins (cert 15)
Magical, classic Swedish gem from director Ingmar Bergman. A 14th-century knight, *Max von Sydow*, plays chess with Death and gets an insight into life.

....

★★★ The Stolen Children 1993   112 mins (cert 15)
Tragic but heartwarming true story about two children growing up on an immigrant's housing estate near Milan.

....

★★★ The Story of Qui Ju 1993   100 mins (cert 12)
Gong Li is splendid in this absorbing, sometimes amusing story of a Chinese village woman's stubborn fight for justice. The overview of modern China is perhaps a little rosy but still very unusual.

....

★★★ Subway 1985   104 mins (cert 15)
Stylish French thriller by Luc Besson about a thief, *Christopher Lambert*, hiding out among the strange community living in the Paris Metro.

....

★★★ Sweet Emma, Dear Bobe 1992   81 mins (cert 18)
Modern Hungary seen through the eyes of two young teachers struggling to make ends meet, and keep their self-respect, in Budapest.

★★★ **Tatie Danielle** 1991   112 mins (cert 15)
Delightful French comedy veers to the black as embittered
widow, *Tsilla Chelton*, exorcises her anger on those around her.

★★★★★ **Throne of Blood** 1957   105 mins (cert 15)
Akira Kurosawa's masterly version of 'Macbeth' in a Samurai
setting. A truly great movie.

★★★ **Tie Me Up! Tie Me Down!** 1989   102 mins (cert 18)
Decidedly kinky effort from Pedro Almodovar about psychiatric
patient *Antonio Banderas*' bizarre efforts to woo a porn star,
Victoria Abril.

★★★★★ **Tokyo Story** 1953   135 mins (cert U)
Elderly Chinese couple travel from rural home to big city to see
children. Greed and generation gap explored by late great
director Yasujiro Ozu.

★★★★ **Toto the Hero** 1991   90 mins (cert 15)
Belgian comedy/drama. Elderly Toto, believing he was given to
wrong parents, seeks revenge for lost, wasted life.

★★★ **Tous les Matins du Monde** 1993   114 mins (cert 12)
Baroque 17th-century musical drama of love and betrayal
starring *Gerard Depardieu* and his son *Guillame*.

★★★ **Trop Belle Pour Toi!** 1989   91 mins (cert 18)
Gerard Depardieu in bittersweet tale of husband who chooses
homely mistress over beautiful wife.

★★ **Les Visiteurs** 1994   100 mins (cert 15)
Wacky French comedy about a 12th-century knight and his
servant who are mistakenly sent into the present day. Probably
funny in French but not in subtitles.

★★★ **The Wedding Banquet** 1993   107 mins (cert 15)
Charming Chinese comedy/drama about a gay man's marriage
of convenience to please his parents. Complications ensue when
he accidentally impregnates the bride.

★★★★ **Wild Strawberries** 1957   93 mins (cert 15)
Victor Sjostrom gives wonderful performance as aged academic
who relives and comes to terms with his life while travelling
across Sweden in this Ingmar Bergman classic.

★★★★ **Women on the Verge
of a Nervous Breakdown** 1988   89 mins   (cert 15)
Glamorous, sexy Spanish farce of a pregnant soap opera star
dumped by her long-term lover.

★★★★ **Yojimbo** 1961   110 mins   (cert PG)
Classic samurai film with bodyguard *Toshiro Mifune* selling his
services to the highest bidder. Used as model for 'A Fistful of
Dollars'.

★★★ **Zéro de Conduite** 1933   47 mins   (cert U)
Surrealist short film about boys' rebellion in a repressive
French boarding school.

HORROR

★★ **After Midnight** 1989   100 mins (cert 18)
Four unimpressive, violent tales in which a college psychology
cast conjure up the things they find scary.

★★★★ **An American Werewolf in London** 1981   97 mins (cert 18)
Brilliant use of soundtrack to indicate numerous changes of
pace in cracking, tongue-in-cheek horror movie by John Landis.

★ **Army of Darkness: The Medieval Dead** 1993   89 mins (cert 15)
Final part of director Sam Raimi's 'Evil Dead' trilogy. Time
travel caper with too little horror, too much tongue-in-cheek.

★★★ **The Birds** 1963   120 mins (cert 15)
Tippi Hedren (Melanie Griffith's mum) stars as the lonely young
woman attacked by killer birds in Alfred Hitchcock's shocker.
Not one of Hitch's very best but it could put you off feeding the
dickies.

★ **Braindead** 1992   104 mins (cert 18)
Schlock horror so bad it's almost enjoyable. Tyrannical zombie
mother won't let her lad date. Nearly as much blood and gore
as 'The Texas Chainsaw Massacre' but a lot more humour.

★★★ **Bram Stoker's Dracula** 1992   123 mins (cert 18)
Coppola's gothic, loyal adaptation. *Gary Oldman* longs to have a
nibble at the neck of *Winona Ryder*. *Anthony Hopkins* – as Van
Helsing – intends to stop him. Beautiful direction, great star
performances and much visual splendour.

★ **Candyman** 1992   93 mins (cert 18)
Silly slasher movie-cum-modern-day ghost story about a vicious
long-dead killer stalking *Virginia Madsen*.

★★★ **Cape Fear** 1961   101 mins (cert 15)
Robert Mitchum gives menacing performance as sadistic ex-con
threatening the lives of lawyer, *Gregory Peck*, and his family.

★★★ **Cape Fear** 1991   127 mins (cert 18)
Robert De Niro seeks revenge on lawyer *Nick Nolte* and family in
Martin Scorsese's violent, horrifying and brilliant movie,
marred by over the top Hollywood ending.

★★ **Carnosaur** 1993   83 mins (cert 15)
Tale of dinosaurs from schlock-horror king Roger Corman. A doctor plans to wipe out the human race in favour of prehistoric creatures.

★★★ **Carrie** 1976   97 mins (cert 18)
Lonesome, creepy child, *Sissy Spacek*, unleashes telekinetic powers against those who wronged her. Shock-horror ending is screen classic.

★★ **Cat People** 1982   118 mins (cert 18)
Nastassja Kinski (and whatever did happen to her?) not at all bad in remake of classic 1943 horror story of a woman who becomes a leopard when she makes love.

★ **Child's Play** 1988   87 mins (cert 15)
Sinister doll possessed by spirit of dead murderer in violent, sometimes amusing, but basically distasteful chiller. (The sequels, 'Child's Play 2' and '3', are even less good.)

★★ **The Church** 1993   98 mins (cert 18)
Evil secrets hidden for years by a cathedral built on the site of a slaughtered ancient village of witches – until now.

★★ **The Dark Half** 1993   121 mins (cert 18)
Timothy Hutton as a novelist whose dead twin is reanimated to persuade him to write again. Directed by George Romero, it also stars *Amy Madigan*.

★★ **The Devils** 1970   111 mins (cert 18)
17th-century nuns apparently possessed by devil. Ken Russell's once controversial, sexy shocker. Probably underrated in its time.

★★★ **Dial M for Murder** 1954   105 mins (cert PG)
Hitchcock at his most teasing. *Ray Milland* as the conniving husband of tormented *Grace Kelly*.

★★★ **Don't Look Now** 1973   110 mins (cert 18)
Julie Christie and *Donald Sutherland* haunted by visions of dead daughter in Nicolas Roeg's much-admired psychological thriller.

★★★ **Dracula** 1979   109 mins (cert 15)

Lush, romantic but rather rambling version of the old vampire story. *Frank Langella* is a sexy Dracula, *Laurence Olivier* a rather hammy Van Helsing.

....

★★ **Eraserhead** 1976   89 mins (cert 18)

David Lynch's weird feature debut in which *John Nance* struggles to come to terms with a mutant child. Not really for the squeamish.

....

★★★★ **The Exorcist** 1973   122 mins (cert 18)

One of the very best tales of demonic possession. *Linda Blair* as the possessed child; *Max von Sydow* the priest wrestling for her soul. Watch for the moment when Blair's head swivels on her shoulders. (Neither of the two sequels matches up.)

....

★★ **The Fly** 1986   96 mins (cert 18)

Jeff Goldblum metamorphosizes into dipterous insect in David Cronenberg's snappy remake. Special effects and touches of humour make it a watchable horror.

....

★ **Freddy's Dead: The Final Nightmare** 1991   90 mins (cert 18)

Sixth and last in the series – thank God. Ten minute 3-D sequence vaguely enlivens this flaccid effort but that's the most that can be said.

....

★★★ **Friday the 13th** 1980   95 mins (cert 18)

Gory slasher-movie. Teenagers slaughtered in summer camp. Loads of gore, very little imagination. Led to umpteen increasingly inept sequels.

....

★★★ **Halloween** 1978   91 mins (cert 18)

First – and best – of the slasher series with *Jamie Lee Curtis* as the babysitter menaced by a mysterious, homicidal lunatic. John Carpenter directed but, alas, he did not direct '2', '3' and '4', which are hardly worth bothering with.

....

★★ **Hellraiser** 1987   93 mins (cert 18)

Gruesome horror from Clive Barker, notable for special effects, about the fiend that lives in the attic and must be fed men's blood. (These films, we suspect, are an acquired taste, which we haven't acquired.)

★★ **Hellraiser II: Hellbound** 1988   93 mins (cert 18)
Ashley Laurence and wicked stepmother *Claire Higgins* battle it out again in the hellish kingdom of the Cenobites. As before, excellent special effects.

★★ **Hellraiser III: Hell on Earth** 1991   92 mins (cert 18)
Better than 'II' but Pin-head and the Cenobites have lost their appeal by now, looking like threatening pin cushions. Still, some interesting ideas and effects explored.

★★ **Henry: Portrait of a Serial Killer** 1991   89 mins (cert 18)
Controversial, ultra-violent, low-budget shocker about a mass murderer. Allegedly based on real life case. Spent a long time awaiting video certification.

★★ **The Hills Have Eyes** 1978   89 mins (cert 18)
Nasty but gripping shocker by Wes Craven in which cannibals eat holidaymakers in the desert. (The sequel – 'The Hills Have Eyes Part II' – also by Craven, is much the same but so feeble that it can only have been made for money.)

★★★★ **The Hitcher** 1986   97 mins (cert 18)
Rutger Hauer hauntingly good as the hitch-hiking psycho preying on the drivers who give him a lift. Some extreme violence and a lot of tension.

★★★ **The Howling** 1981   91 mins (cert 18)
Joe Dante's tongue-in-cheek story (from a John Sayles script) of California community overrun by werewolves. Led to no fewer than five sequels of which 'V: The Rebirth' and 'VI: The Freaks' are better than the rest.)

★★ **Leprechaun** 1993   88 mins (cert 15)
Dan O'Grady discovers an Irish fairy but it doesn't bring much luck with it as the father and daughter take a holiday at the site of its gold.

★★★★ **Misery** 1990   107 mins (cert 18)
Car crash leaves novelist, *James Caan*, imprisoned by number one fan, *Kathy Bates*, in exceptional psychological blood-curdler.

★★★★ **A Nightmare on Elm Street** 1984   91 mins (cert 18)
Wes Craven's teenage nightmare terrifies thanks to the eerie effects and *Robert Englund* as the bogey man. Followed by five sequels, all progressively less good and made by lesser directors.

★ **Nightmare Vacation** 1984   95 mins (cert 18)
A grisly slasher tale about a bunch of young people on holiday being picked off one by one by an unknown killer.

★★ **Night of the Living Dead** 1990   89 mins (cert 18)
George Romero's violent, gruesome, black-and-white story of flesh-eating zombies. If you like ugly this is the film for you.

★★★ **The Omen** 1976   111 mins (cert 18)
Son of *Gregory Peck* and *Lee Remick* turns out to be the Antichrist in a gripping tale of the supernatural. The law of diminishing returns comes into play with all three sequels.

★★ **The People Under the Stairs** 1991   102 mins (cert 18)
Tongue-in-cheek horror from Wes Craven. Black child rescues little girl and other strange inmates from weird house.

★ **Pet Sematary** 1989   102 mins (cert 18)
Family suffers all sorts of nastiness in new home behind Indian burial ground in Steven King nasty. The sequel is no better.

★★ **The Phantom of the Opera** 1989   91 mins (cert 18)
More on the lines of a slasher movie than an attempt to be faithful to the original novel. Well, what would you expect with Elm Street's Freddie – *Robert Englund* – involved?

★★★ **Poltergeist** 1982   114 mins (cert 15)
Scary goings-on when unfriendly spirits invade the home of a nice middle-class family. Nice performances, great effects. Inevitably the spirits returned, to similar effect, in two sequels.

★★★★ **Psycho** 1960   109 mins (cert 15)
Still the best of all shock-horror movies. *Anthony Perkins* as demented Norman Bates in Hitchcock classic.

★★★ **Rosemary's Baby** 1968   137 mins (cert 18)
Mia Farrow suffers psychological torment – and worse – when husband, *John Cassavetes*, becomes involved with Satanic cult in Roman Polanski's supernatural thriller.

★★★★ **The Shining** 1980   146 mins (cert 18)
Jack Nicholson, off-season caretaker at a hotel, goes mad in this overlong but originally underrated Stanley Kubrick chiller. Based on a Stephen King novel.

★★★★★ **The Silence of the Lambs** 1991   119 mins (cert 18)
A violent, shocking and outstanding film. Rookie FBI agent, *Jodie Foster*, hunts a serial killer with the help of incarcerated psychopath, *Anthony Hopkins*. Cleaned up at the Oscars.

 ★★ **Sleepwalkers** 1992   89 mins (cert 18)
Incest between a couple of zombies, mother and son, who need the blood of young virgins to survive. But virgins are pretty thin on the ground these days.

 ★★★ **Tales from the Dark Side** 1990   93 mins (cert 18)
Christian Slater and *Debbie Harry* contribute to four horror stories written by masters of the genre, including Conan Doyle and Stephen King.

 ★★ **The Unholy** 1988   102 mins (cert 18)
Two Roman Catholic priests have been murdered and their successor, *Ben Cross*, discovers nasty Satanic practices in his new parish. Bit daft, bit gory, but quite interesting.

★★★ **Witchboard** 1986   94 mins (cert 15)
A group of young friends run into trouble when they contact the spirit of a mass murderer on their ouija board.

★★★ **The Woman in Black** 1989   99 mins (cert 15)
Truly terrifying ghost story by novelist Susan Hill, cleverly adapted for the screen.

 ★★ **Zombies: Dawn of the Dead** 1979   126 mins (cert 18)
George Romero at it again with a lip-smacking relish of gore as the zombies look like taking over the whole of America.

MUSICALS

★ **Absolute Beginners** 1986   100 mins (cert 15)
Stylish but unsatisfying British musical set in London in the
1950s. Box-office flop in its time. Cast includes *Patsy Kensit*,
James Fox and *David Bowie*.

★★★ **All That Jazz** 1979   123 mins (cert 15)
Imaginative piece starring *Roy Scheider* as choreographer Joe
Gideon working himself into the grave.

★★★ **An American in Paris** 1951   113 mins (cert U)
Pleasing setting with *Gene Kelly*, *Leslie Caron* and Gershwin tunes
in great musical spectacular.

★★★ **Anchors Aweigh** 1945   139 mins (cert U)
All-singing, all-dancing *Gene Kelly* and *Frank Sinatra* as a couple
of sailors enjoying shore leave.

★★★ **The Band Wagon** 1953   112 mins (cert U)
Lively and sophisticated backstage musical with *Fred Astaire*,
Cyd Charisse, *Jack Buchanan* and the song 'That's Entertainment'
among many others.

★★★ **The Barkleys of Broadway** 1949   109 mins (cert U)
Final pairing of *Fred Astaire* and *Ginger Rogers*, themselves
reuniting after ten years, as a showbiz couple who split up and
reunite. Not their best but good, nostalgic stuff.

★★★ **Bird** 1988   154 mins (cert 15)
Clint Eastwood's cool but affectionate look at the life of
legendary jazzman Charlie Parker with *Forest Whitaker* splendid
in the main role.

★★ **Bloodhounds of Broadway** 1989   93 mins (cert PG)
Madonna and *Matt Dillon* in a loose adaptation of a Damon
Runyon story. Lightweight but amusing.

★★ **The Blues Brothers** 1980   113 mins (cert 15)
Brash John Landis comedy with *James Belushi* and *Dan Aykroyd* as
musicians trying to save an orphanage. Great score. It now has
a cult following but who can understand cults?

★★ **Brigadoon** 1954   108 mins (cert U)
Twee but charming musical fantasy with *Gene Kelly* as the
American finding a mythical Scottish village and *Cyd Charisse*.

★★ **The Buddy Holly Story** 1978   113 mins (cert PG)
Soundtrack's the star though *Gary Busey* is competent as the
legendary but ill-fated singer.

★★★ **Cabaret** 1972   123 mins (cert 15)
Liza Minnelli stars in multiple Oscar-winning musical set in pre-
war Nazi Germany. Based on Christopher Isherwood stories.

★★ **Calamity Jane** 1953   101 mins (cert U)
Doris Day as the gun totin' female who must resort to feminine
wiles to win Wild Bill Hickock, *Howard Keel*, in lively Western
musical.

★★★ **Carmen** 1983   102 mins (cert 15)
Life imitates art in Carlos Saura's ingenious story about a
choreographer falling for leading lady as they stage Bizet's
opera.

★★★ **A Chorus Line** 1985   111 mins (cert PG)
Richard Attenborough's underrated but often exhilarating
screen version of the much-admired, long-running stage
musical.

★★ **Chuck Berry: Hail! Hail! Rock and Roll** 1987   120 mins (cert PG)
Documentary about the legendary old singer. A pretty candid
look at his sometimes shocking life and times.

★★★★ **The Commitments** 1991   117 mins (cert 15)
Alan Parker's funny, joyous story of a Dublin soul band, its rise
and fall. A warming paean to the spirit of human optimism.

★★ **Cover Girl** 1944   107 mins (cert U)
Jolly but clichéd comedy with *Rita Hayworth* and *Gene Kelly*,
partly saved by Jerome Kern and Ira Gershwin score.

★★★ **Dirty Dancing** 1987   97 mins (cert 15)
Patrick Swayze hot-hoofs his way into *Jennifer Grey*'s heart in slim
but pleasing rites-of-passage musical.

★★★★ **Easter Parade** 1948   96 mins (cert U)
Lovely Irving Berlin score with *Fred Astaire*, *Judy Garland* and *Ann Miller* in showbiz setting.

★★ **Fame** 1980   133 mins (cert PG)
New York school of performing arts is the setting for Alan Parker's vibrant musical drama which spawned a successful TV spinoff.

★★ **Fiddler on the Roof** 1971   181 mins (cert U)
Nostalgic tale of a father, *Topol*, clinging to old Jewish values and trying to marry off his daughters in changing Russia.

★★ **Flashdance** 1983   96 mins (cert 15)
Young *Jennifer Beals* dreams of making the big time as a dancer in pretty daft Adrian Lyne movie, saved by good dance sequences.

★★★★ **42nd Street** 1933   89 mins (cert U)
Warner Baxter and *Ruby Keeler* in the definitive musical about the understudy who comes back a star.

★★ **Funny Face** 1957   103 mins (cert U)
Gershwin score enhances this charming musical romance with *Fred Astaire* discovering talents of *Audrey Hepburn*.

★★ **Funny Girl** 1968   169 mins (cert U)
Touching biopic with a roller-skating *Barbra Streisand* playing Ziegfield Follies star Fanny Brice.

★★ **Gigi** 1958   119 mins (cert PG)
'Thank heaven for little girls' – musical gem with ravishing *Leslie Caron* more interested in *Louis Jourdan* than becoming a courtesan.

★★★ **The Glenn Miller Story** 1954   116 mins (cert U)
James Stewart's warm and convincing portrayal of the famed band leader.

★★ **Grease** 1978   110 mins (cert PG)
Bland story of young love enhanced by great Bee Gees songs and enthusiastic performances from *John Travolta* and *Olivia Newton John*.

★★★ **Hair** 1979   121 mins (cert 15)
The famous 1960s stage musical filmed well by Milos Forman
but perhaps a decade too late to have much significance.

★★★ **A Hard Day's Night** 1964   83 mins (cert U)
The *Beatles*' first film and their best. An ingenious, black-and-
white fantasy, endearingly concocted by director Richard
Lester.

★★ **Hello, Dolly!** 1969   146 mins (cert U)
Gene Kelly directs *Barbra Streisand* as a meddling matchmaker
in a period piece that doesn't reach expectations.

★★★★ **High Society** 1956   107 mins (cert U)
Lovely musical version of 'The Philadelphia story' with *Grace
Kelly*, *Frank Sinatra*, *Bing Crosby* and Cole Porter songs – what
more could you ask for?

★★★ **Holiday Inn** 1942   101 mins (cert U)
Romantic tale notable for *Bing Crosby*'s rendition of 'White
Christmas'. *Fred Astaire* provides nifty footwork and Irving
Berlin some great songs.

★★ **In Bed with Madonna** 1991   119 mins (cert 18)
Self-indulgent peep at musical megastar on tour. Concert
footage redeems some of the overt silliness.

★★ **Jesus Christ Superstar** 1973   103 mins (cert PG)
Innovative Andrew Lloyd Webber and Tim Rice stage hit
brought entertainingly to screen by Norman Jewison.

★★ **The Jolson Story** 1946   129 mins (cert U)
Al Jolson sings but *Larry Parks* acts in this biopic of the great
vaudeville and Broadway singer. (The sequel – 'Jolson Sings
Again' – is less good.)

★★★★ **The King and I** 1956   133 mins (cert U)
Rogers and Hammerstein charmer set in the court of Siam.
Governess, *Deborah Kerr*, instructs royal children and falls for
king, *Yul Brynner*. Packed with splendid set pieces.

★★★★ **Kiss Me Kate** 1953   111 mins (cert U)
Great Cole Porter frolic loosely based on 'The Taming of the
Shrew'. *Ann Miller*, *Howard Keel* and *Ann Blyth* on brilliant form.

★★ **La Bamba** 1987   108 mins (cert 15)
Competent biopic about popster Ritchie Valens who made the
fatal mistake of hitching a ride in Buddy Holly's plane.

....

★★★ **Meet Me in St Louis** 1944   113 mins (cert U)
Heartwarming *Judy Garland* vehicle based on a year in the life of
a family during the St Louis World Fair, 1903.

....

★★★ **The Music Man** 1962   151 mins (cert U)
Rousing musical about salesman-cum-conartist, *Robert Preston*,
who arrives in a small town to form a brass band.

....

★★★★ **My Fair Lady** 1964   175 mins (cert U)
Audrey Hepburn as the Victorian flower girl turned into a lady by
professor *Rex Harrison*. Lovely score, design and costumes.

....

★★★ **New York, New York** 1977   137 mins (cert PG)
Saxophonist *Robert De Niro* and singer *Liza Minnelli* love and
squabble through the Big Band era in Martin Scorsese's
effective but over-ambitious movie.

....

★★★★ **Oklahoma!** 1955   145 mins (cert U)
Rogers and Hammerstein again. *Shirley Jones* is the country girl
pursued by cowboy *Gordon MacRae* and evil farmhand *Rod Steiger*.

....

★★★★ **Oliver!** 1968   146 mins (cert U)
Lavish musical version of 'Oliver Twist'. *Mark Lester* cute as
Oliver, *Ron Moody* splendid as Fagin. Great score and
choreography.

....

★★★ **On the Town** 1949   98 mins (cert U)
Exuberant yarn about three sailors – *Gene Kelly*, *Frank Sinatra*
and *Jules Munshin* – finding romance and adventure on 24-hour
leave in New York.

....

★★★ **The Pajama Game** 1957   101 mins (cert U)
Rousing musical romance with *Doris Day* heading factory
workers' demands for pay rise but falling for boss.

....

★★ **Pal Joey** 1957   112 mins (cert U)
Charming, libidinous heel *Frank Sinatra* uses women – *Kim
Novak* and *Rita Hayworth* – in bid to build his own night club.
Great songs, slim story.

★★ **Pink Floyd: The Wall** 1982 95 mins (cert 15)
Alan Parker's affectionate visualization of band's best-selling album. *Bob Hoskins* and *Bob Geldof* appear.

★★★ **The Pirates of Penzance** 1983 112 mins (cert U)
Colourful, lively movie of Gilbert and Sullivan's operetta. *Kevin Kline* adds sex appeal.

★★★ **Quadrophenia** 1979 120 mins (cert 18)
Mods and Rockers fight it out on Britain's beaches. *Sting* makes strong impression in acting debut.

★★★ **Round Midnight** 1986 131 mins (cert 15)
Bertrand Tavernier's loving homage to great jazz musicians, Bud Powell and Lester Young. Nice score from Herbie Hancock.

★★ **Sarafina** 1992 166 mins (cert 15)
Musical set in Soweto township where the children rose against apartheid and were massacred. *Whoopi Goldberg* as teacher. Nice songs and choreography, but would have been better shorter.

★★ **Saturday Night Fever** 1977 119 mins (cert 18)
Catchy tunes, nice dance numbers and a plot about a young Italian, *John Travolta*, who lives to dance until love shows him there is more to life.

★★★★ **Seven Brides for Seven Brothers** 1954 104 mins (cert U)
Delightful songs plus some of best choreography ever staged. *Jane Powell* as the young bride making a home for *Howard Keel* and his six brothers.

★★★★ **Show Boat** 1951 108 mins (cert U)
Splendid weepy set on the Mississippi. Heartbreak and romance for *Howard Keel*, *Kathryn Grayson* and *Ava Gardner* to the strains of Jerome Kern's beautiful score.

★★★★★ **Singin' in the Rain** 1952 102 mins (cert U)
Quite simply the best of all musicals. Great dancing by *Gene Kelly* and *Donald O'Connor*.

★★★★ **The Sound of Music** 1965 172 mins (cert U)
Sentimental saga about a convent girl, *Julie Andrews*, becoming nanny to large family in pre-war Austria. Wonderful songs.

MUSICALS ■

★★★★ South Pacific 1958   170 mins (cert U)
Exotic Rogers and Hammerstein musical of WWII life on a Pacific island. Songs include 'Nothing Like a Dame' and 'Happy Talk'.

★★★ That'll Be the Day 1974   91 mins (cert 15)
Young lads in 1950s England use rock music to escape their humdrum lives. Stars *David Essex* and *Ringo Starr*. Dated but enjoyable.

★★★★ That's Entertainment 1974   132 mins (cert U)
A loving eulogy to the best of MGM's musicals narrated by its stars and featuring a montage of the studio's greatest hits.

★★★ That's Entertainment Part II 1976   133 mins (cert U)
More of the same, only not quite so much fun. *Fred Astaire* and *Gene Kelly* link the excerpts.

★★★★ Top Hat 1935   100 mins (cert U)
Wonderful songs and nifty footwork lift the usual, mistaken-identity plot in *Fred Astaire* and *Ginger Rogers* romance.

★★★ U2 – Rattle and Hum 1988   99 mins (cert 15)
Pretty good documentary of the Irish band's 1987 tour, the concerts nicely balanced by backstage stuff about visits to Harlem and Graceland.

★★★ West Side Story 1961   155 mins (cert U)
'Romeo and Juliet' set to music in modern-day, gangland America. *Natalie Wood* and *Richard Beymer* are the lovers from opposing gangs.

★★★ White Christmas 1954   120 mins (cert U)
Army pals, *Bing Crosby* and *Danny Kaye*, try to boost popularity of holiday resort, aided by Irving Berlin's score.

★★ Woodstock 1970   184 mins (cert U)
Seminal documentary of the famous weekend rock festival. Great footage of the *Who*, *Jimi Hendrix*, *Joe Cocker*, *Sly and the Family Stone* and others. Now rich in historical value.

★★★ Yankee Doodle Dandee 1942   126 mins (cert U)
James Cagney great as song-and-dance man-cum-playwright, George M Cohan, in lavish biography.

MYSTERY/THRILLER

⋆⋆ **Absence of Malice** 1981   161 mins (cert PG)
Journalist *Sally Field* is duped into writing story that discredits
innocent and angry *Paul Newman*. Crisp examination of press
corruption.

⋆⋆ **Altered States** 1980   102 mins (cert 18)
Roller-coaster psychological study of scientist, *William Hurt*.
Typical flamboyant direction by Ken Russell.

⋆⋆ **The Anderson Tapes** 1972   98 mins (cert PG)
Fast-moving thriller in which *Sean Connery* attempts to pull off
major heist under police surveillance.

⋆⋆⋆ **Angel Heart** 1987   113 mins (cert 18)
Heart-stopping tension created by director Alan Parker. *Mickey
Rourke* takes on *Robert De Niro* as the devil in a suspense thriller
not for the faint-hearted.

⋆ **Another Stakeout** 1993   109 mins (cert PG)
Emilio Estevez and *Richard Dreyfuss* find themselves playing happy
families with assistant DA *Rosie O'Donnell* as they seek to find a
witness before the Mob gets her. Silly sequel not worth waiting
six years for.

⋆⋆⋆ **Bad Day at Black Rock** 1954   78 mins (cert PG)
Spencer Tracy encounters hostility in desert town when looking
for missing Japanese farmer after WWII.

⋆ **Basic Instinct** 1992   128 mins (cert 18)
Michael Douglas and *Sharon Stone* in violent, well-made but trashy
anti-feminist thriller with women shown as objects of fantasy or
fear. Stone's notorious flash doesn't come over so clearly (thank
God) on video.

⋆⋆ **The Bedroom Window** 1987   112 mins (cert 15)
Intriguing though over-plotted thriller. Illicit lovers *Steve
Guttenberg* and *Elizabeth McGovern* unwittingly involved in murder
investigation.

★★ **Bellman and True** 1988   121 mins (cert 15)
Realistic suspense story of computer expert forced to aid
robbery when his son is kidnapped. Fine performance by
Bernard Hill.

....

★ **Benefit of the Doubt** 1993   92 mins (cert 18)
Daughter gives evidence at father's murder trial; 27 years later
he's back in her life. *Donald Sutherland* and *Amy Irving* play not-
so-happy families in a sloppily written, sloppily directed
melodrama.

....

★★ **Best Seller** 1987   95 mins (cert 18)
Uneasy, unbelievable, but engaging story of author/cop, *Brian
Dennehy*, appointed by hitman, *James Woods*, to stir up a viper's
nest of corruption.

....

★★ **Betrayed** 1988   126 mins (cert 18)
FBI agent, *Debra Winger*, romantically involved with redneck
racist *Tom Berenger*. Love blurs her judgement in investigation of
KKK activities.

....

★★★ **The Big Easy** 1987   108 mins (cert 18)
Offbeat New Orleans cop *Dennis Quaid* and uptight but sexy DA
Ellen Barkin investigate a case of police corruption. All very
spicy and enjoyable.

....

★★★ **The Big Heat** 1953   90 mins (cert 15)
Fritz Lang's notable piece of film noir about a policeman, *Glenn
Ford*, going undercover to get revenge on a crime ring. *Lee
Marvin*, as the killer, is as sadistic as only he could be.

....

★★★★★ **The Big Sleep** 1944   99 mins (cert PG)
Howard Hawks directs *Humphrey Bogart* and *Lauren Bacall* in a
convoluted investigation of sex and murder. Confusing but
terrific and quite the best of all the Philip Marlowe movies.

....

★★ **Bitter Moon** 1992   139 mins (cert 18)
Roman Polanski's steamy, sexy melodrama set aboard a cruise
liner. Crippled *Peter Coyote* manipulates *Emmanuelle Seigner* and
Hugh Grant. More preposterous than erotic.

....

★★ **Black Rain** 1989   125 mins (cert 18)
Ridley Scott's violent cops and robbers thriller set in Japan is
tough, long and predictable. *Michael Douglas* and *Andy Garcia*
can't save it from obscurity.

★★ **Black Widow** 1986   103 mins (cert 15)
Debra Winger as an FBI agent on the trail of husband-killer
Theresa Russell in Bob Rafelson's steamy thriller.

★★ **Blood Simple** 1984   98 mins (cert 18)
John Getz hires private eye *Emmett Walsh* to spy on his wife in
Coen brothers' much-admired but deeply flawed debut film.

★★★ **Blow Out** 1981   108 mins (cert 18)
Brian De Palma's sexy thriller about a sound effects man, *John
Travolta*, innocently taping a murder. Good suspense, neat
twists and turns.

★ **Blue Ice** 1992   105 mins (cert 15)
A really dopey thriller set in London and hardly helped by the
romantic pairing of *Michael Caine* and *Sean Young*, who belong to
very different generations.

★★ **Blue Velvet** 1986   120 mins (cert 18)
David Lynch's stylish, nasty story of small-town corruption and
violence. *Dennis Hopper*'s psycho steals the show. Another cult
movie.

★★★ **Body Heat** 1981   113 mins (cert 18)
Lawrence Kasdan's sweaty, erotic conspiracy in which *William
Hurt* and *Kathleen Turner* plot to kill her husband.

★ **Body of Evidence** 1992   99 mins (cert 18)
Madonna's accused of murdering her lover through sex.
Seducing her lawyer, *Willem Dafoe*, ensures she gets the best
defence. Sex scenes are totally risible. Use of candle wax and
crushed light bulbs makes the eyes water.

★ **Boiling Point** 1993   92 mins (cert 15)
US agent *Wesley Snipes* on trail of counterfeiters who murdered
his partner. *Dennis Hopper* and *Viggo Mortenson* co-star in a flat,
unimaginative thriller.

★★★ **Brighton Rock** 1947   91 mins (cert PG)
Excellent version of Graham Greene's psychological thriller.
Richard Attenborough found stardom as Pinkie.

★★★★ **Bullitt** 1968   113 mins (cert U)
Steve McQueen at his best in police drama memorable for San
Francisco car chase that spawned many imitators.

★★★ **Carlito's Way** 1993   108 mins (cert 15)
Al Pacino on top form as legendary Puerto Rican crook trying to go straight in hostile New York environment in Brian De Palma's crackling thriller.

....

★★★ **Cat Chaser** 1989   98 mins (cert 18)
Pretty fair adaptation of Elmore Leonard thriller with *Peter Weller* and *Kelly McGillis* making up for Abel Ferrara's clumsy direction.

....

★★★ **The China Syndrome** 1979   122 mins (cert PG)
Accident at nuclear power station and subsequent cover up provide meaty roles for *Jane Fonda* and *Michael Douglas*.

....

★★★★ **Chinatown** 1974   131 mins (cert 18)
Faye Dunaway hires private eye, *Jack Nicholson*, to investigate skulduggery in Roman Polanski's tense, riveting mystery set in 1930s LA. A modern classic.

....

★ **Close to Eden** 1993   110 mins (cert 15)
Melanie Griffith unbelievable as cop investigating murder among New York's reclusive Hasidic Jews. Sidney Lumet directed but it's hard to see why.

....

★★★ **Compromising Positions** 1985   98 mins (cert 15)
Housewife *Susan Sarandon* gets involved in a lively, amusing murder investigation led by detective *Raul Julia* when her dentist is killed.

....

★★ **Consenting Adults** 1992   100 mins (cert 15)
Kevin Kline regrets sleeping with neighbour's wife when framed for her murder. First half keeps you gripped, second half barely keeps you awake.

....

★★ **Conspiracy** 1989   87 mins (cert 18)
Muddled thriller about a secret agent sent to hush up scandal in the Pentagon. *James Wilby* stars.

....

★★★ **The Conversation** 1974   113 mins (cert 15)
Excellent Francis Coppola story of surveillance operator, *Gene Hackman*, becoming personally involved in case of murder.

....

★★ **Criminal Justice** 1990   90 mins (cert 15)
Courtroom drama notable for *Forest Whitaker*'s performance as black defendant accused of mugging unsavoury young woman.

★★ **Criminal Law** 1989   117 mins (cert 18)
Weakly plotted story of attorney's dilemma when his acquitted
client plans to kill again. With *Kevin Bacon* and *Gary Oldman*.

★★ **The Crush** 1993   89 mins (cert 15)
Cary Elwes finds life becomes a nightmare when 14-year-old girl
develops a fatal crush on him. *Jennifer Rubin* is his long suffering
girlfriend.

★ **Crush** 1993   96 mins (cert 15)
Set in New Zealand where a car crash leaves one girl seriously
injured and lends an opportunity for another to take advantage
of her absence with a reclusive novelist. Unconvincing tale of
revenge.

★★ **The Darkman** 1990   91 mins (cert 15)
Violence proves no substitute for plot in feeble thriller about
disfigured scientist, *Liam Neeson*, wreaking revenge.

★★★ **Dead Again** 1991   101 mins (cert 15)
Complex, intriguing plot providing dual roles for husband and
wife team, *Emma Thompson* and *Kenneth Branagh*, not to mention
juicy parts for *Derek Jacobi* and *Andy Garcia*.

★ **Dead-Bang** 1989   102 mins (cert 18)
Don Johnson is a cop in this convoluted, unconvincing thriller
involving neo-Nazis and *Penelope Ann Miller*.

★★★ **Dead Calm** 1989   95 mins (cert 15)
Mystery and mayhem aboard hijacked yacht with *Sam Neill* and
Nicole Kidman. *Billy Zane* steals the show as psycho killer.

★★★ **The Deadly Affair** 1967   106 mins (cert 15)
Sidney Lumet's web of espionage starring *James Mason* as the
prototype George Smiley investigating colleague's suicide.
Based on John Le Carré novel.

★★ **Deadly Pursuit** 1988   110 mins (cert 15)
Killer at large in mountain expedition led by *Kirstie Alley*
pursued by detective *Sidney Poitier* and *Tom Berenger*. Known as
'Shoot to Kill' in USA.

★★★ **Deceived** 1991   108 mins (cert 15)
Goldie Hawn discovers to her peril that her late husband, *John
Heard*, had a double life. Nicely done.

★★ **Deep Cover** 1992   112 mins (cert 18)
Larry Fishburne as narcotics cop working so deeply undercover with drug dealer *Jeff Goldblum* no one's sure which side he's on. Not bad but could have been snappier.

★★★ **Defence of the Realm** 1985   96 mins (cert PG)
Government cover-up forms basis of British political conspiracy and murder story with *Gabriel Byrne* and *Denholm Elliott*.

★★ **The Desperate Hours** 1990   105 mins (cert 15)
Michael Cimino's violent but dullish remake features *Mickey Rourke* as escaped psycho holing up with hostages *Anthony Hopkins* and family.

★★ **Diary of a Hitman** 1991   102 mins (cert 18)
Forest Whitaker is a hitman gone soft when sent to kill *Sherilyn Fenn* and baby. Brief appearance by *Sharon Stone* – no, she keeps her clothes on. Whitaker too good for this inconsequential type of thriller.

★★ **DOA** 1988   98 mins (cert 15)
When *Dennis Quaid* discovers he's been poisoned with only 24 hours to live, he and *Meg Ryan* go after the killer. Good start, bad ending.

★★ **Double Jeopardy** 1993   97 mins (cert 18)
Rachel Ward is the ex-girlfriend disrupting the life of *Bruce Boxleitner*. Too heavy on violence and too light on plot to be an effective erotic thriller.

★★ **Dressed to Kill** 1980   104 mins (cert 18)
Brian De Palma's sexy, sometimes distasteful thriller has killer stalking *Angie Dickinson* and *Nancy Allen*. *Michael Caine* also stars.

★★★★ **Duel** 1971   85 mins (cert PG)
Tense stuff as mild motorist, *Dennis Weaver*, is persecuted by oil-truck driver. Steven Spielberg's first film shows filmmaking at its best.

★★ **Electra Glide in Blue** 1973   113 mins (cert 18)
Well-plotted, violent thriller. *Robert Blake* rises from diminutive status as traffic cop to plain-clothes detective on a murder hunt.

★★ **Everybody Wins** 1990   98 mins (cert 15)
Nick Nolte and *Debra Winger* in convoluted, tiresome plot by Arthur Miller in which Nolte investigates a murky web of corruption.

★★ **Family Business** 1986   110 mins (cert 15)
Despite a cast which includes *Sean Connery*, *Dustin Hoffman* and *Matthew Broderick*, this comic thriller about a family of burglars falls flat.

★★★ **Fatal Attraction** 1987   119 mins (cert 18)
Glenn Close as obsessed, spurned mistress wreaking revenge on *Michael Douglas* and family. Gripping but overblown.

★★ **Fatal Beauty** 1987   104 mins (cert 18)
Whoopi Goldberg as Beverly Hills cop going underground to nab a cocaine ring. So-so but a failure as an attempted 'Beverly Hills Cop' seen from the distaff side.

★★ **Fatal Vision** 1984   108 mins (cert 15)
Murder/mystery based on true story of American doctor accused of murdering wife and daughters. *Karl Malden* splendid as man seeking justice.

★ **Femme Fatale** 1991   96 mins (cert 15)
Newlywed's wife mysteriously vanishes in thriller starring *Billy Zane* and *Colin Firth*. Doesn't amount to much. Billy's sister, *Liza Zane*, plays the bride.

★★★ **Final Analysis** 1991   125 mins (cert 15)
Psychiatrist *Richard Gere* gets involved with his patient *Uma Thurman*'s sister, *Kim Basinger*, but finds he's bitten off more than he can chew in a knife-edge thriller wherein no woman is quite what she seems.

★★★ **The Firm** 1993   155 mins (cert 15)
Tom Cruise as new lawyer in a firm laundering money for the Mob faces tricky quandary: to play ball with the FBI and risk losing his career or condone the corruption. *Gene Hackman*, *Holly Hunter* and *Ed Harris* co-star.

★★ **Flatliners** 1990   114 mins (cert 15)
Five medical students experiment with the after life. Despite decent cast, including *Kiefer Sutherland*, *Kevin Bacon* and *Julia Roberts*, both dark and comic moments fall flat.

★★★ **Frantic** 1988   120 mins (cert 15)
Hit-and-miss mystery by Roman Polanski in which *Harrison Ford*
and *Emmanuelle Seigner* search Paris for his missing wife.

....

★★★ **The French Connection** 1971   104 mins (cert 18)
Narcotics cops, *Gene Hackman* and *Roy Scheider*, fighting heroin
importers in NY. Good action movie with exceptional car chase.

....

★★★ **The French Connection II** 1975   119 mins (cert 18)
Gene Hackman reprises his role of Popeye Doyle – this time in
Paris – in acceptable sequel.

....

★★ **Gleaming the Cube** 1989   105 mins (cert PG)
Silly murder/mystery for teenage *Christian Slater* to investigate
on his skateboard. Stunts make it worth watching.

....

★★★ **The Good Son** 1993   115 mins (cert 15)
In which 13-year-old multi-millionaire *Macaulay Culkin* plays the
bad guy for the first time. A nice idea ineptly worked out.

....

★★★ **Gorky Park** 1983   102 mins (cert 15)
Intriguing spy story set in the last days of the Cold War. With
William Hurt as the Moscow cop investigating murder.

....

★★ **Guilty As Sin** 1993   99 mins (cert 15)
Rebecca De Mornay as hot-shot defence lawyer hired to defend
smooth wife-killer *Don Johnson* – only to find her life threatened
by her terrifying client.

....

★★★★ **The Hand That Rocks the Cradle** 1992   110 mins (cert 15)
Rebecca De Mornay as a revengeful nanny gradually reducing
Anabella Sciorra's happy family life to ashes in nail-biting,
sinister thriller.

....

★★★ **The Hard Way** 1989   111 mins (cert 15)
Movie star, *Michael J Fox*, attaches himself to unwelcoming
hard-nosed cop, *James Woods*, to research a forthcoming role.
Lovely performances and a lot of fun to watch.

....

★★ **The Hawk** 1993   86 mins (cert 15)
Helen Mirren fears her husband's the serial killer at large since
her hammer is missing! She is good, the rest of the film
disappoints.

★★★★ Hidden Agenda 1990   108 mins (cert 15)
Ken Loach's palm-sweating thriller focusing upon the British
government's dirty tricks in Northern Ireland. *Brian Cox* leads
an excellent cast.

★★★ Homicide 1991   102 mins (cert 18)
Jewish cop *Joe Mantegna* finds his loyalties are divided when he
investigates sinister murder of Jewish pawn shop owner in
David Mamet's grim, thoughtful thriller.

★★ The Hot Spot 1990   130 mins (cert 18)
Steamy and atmospheric conspiracy story. *Don Johnson* and
Virginia Madsen as ne'er-do-wells who deserve each other in hot
southern town.

★★ House of Cards 1992   105 mins (cert 15)
Strange psychological drama about disturbed young girl's brush
with the supernatural after her father dies. *Kathleen Turner* is
the mother reluctantly accepting help from psychiatrist *Tommy
Lee Jones*.

★★★ House of Games 1987   102 mins (cert 15)
David Mamet's ingenious tale of psychiatrist embroiled in web
of mystery when she helps a conman patient. With *Lindsay
Crouse* and *Joe Mantegna*.

★★ Indecent Proposal 1992   117 mins (cert 15)
In which billionaire *Robert Redford* offers $1 million for a night
with *Demi Moore* to prove to her and hubby, *Woody Harrelson*, that
money can buy anything. Hardly seems worth it. Tears before
bedtime are guaranteed.

★★★ Internal Affairs 1990   114 mins (cert 18)
Crooked cop *Richard Gere* is investigated by fellow officer, *Andy
Garcia*, in tough, convincing action/drama.

★★★★ In the Heat of the Night 1967   109 mins (cert 15)
Bigoted southern sheriff *Rod Steiger* grudgingly accepts help of
big city black cop, *Sidney Poitier*, in murder investigation. A very
superior thriller.

★★ The Ipcress File 1965   109 mins (cert PG)
Michael Caine's first and best outing as Len Deighton's Cockney
secret agent, Harry Palmer.

★★★ **Jacob's Ladder** 1990   113 mins (cert 18)
Psychological drama with *Tim Robbins* as a Vietnam veteran
discovering source of his terrifying hallucinations. Full of
interesting ideas but cops out at the end.

★★★★ **Jagged Edge** 1985   108 mins (cert 18)
Excellent, tense did-he, didn't-he suspense thriller. *Jeff Bridges* is
the man accused of murdering his wife, *Glenn Close* the lawyer
defending and sleeping with him.

★★ **Jennifer Eight** 1992   124 mins (cert 15)
Andy Garcia as ex-LA cop finding new job and a severed hand in
new town where a killer's preying on blind woman *Uma Thurman*.

★★ **Johnny Handsome** 1989   94 mins (cert 15)
Unusual Walter Hill crime story in which disfigured *Mickey
Rourke* gets a new face and plans revenge on *Ellen Barkin* and
others who double-crossed him.

★★★ **Jumpin' Jack Flash** 1986   100 mins (cert 15)
Whoopi Goldberg as computer operator embroiled in espionage.
Neat outlet for her comic flair.

★★ **Keeper of the City** 1992   114 mins (cert 15)
Lou Gossett Jr as troubled cop hunting vigilante killer, *Anthony La
Paglia*.

★★★ **Key Largo** 1948   101 mins (cert PG)
Gangster *Edward G Robinson* holds *Humphrey Bogart*, *Lauren Bacall*
and others captive in John Huston film noir. Wordy but nicely
world-weary.

★★ **Kill Me Again** 1989   96 mins (cert 18)
Violent but stylish thriller with *Val Kilmer* as a Reno private eye
and *Joanne Whalley-Kilmer* (his wife) as a steamy femme fatale. A
much better than average mystery tale.

★★ **A Kiss Before Dying** 1991   92 mins (cert 18)
Psychopath *Matt Dillon* uses wife, *Sean Young*, to achieve greedy
ambitions. Poor remake of goodish 1956 movie.

★★★ **Klute** 1971   140 mins (cert 18)
Everyone's dream hooker *Jane Fonda* is menaced by a
psychopath. *Donald Sutherland* as the helpful cop in a tense,
first-rate thriller.

★★ **The Lady in White** 1989   103 mins (cert 15)
Eerie and enjoyable thriller in which *Lukas Haas* (the kid from 'Witness') is threatened by a strangler when his friends lock him in school as a Halloween prank.

★★★ **The Late Show** 1977   93 mins (cert 15)
Excellent, witty, well-plotted murder mystery. *Art Carnie* as the aged private eye, *Lily Tomlin* his infuriating client.

★★★★ **Laura** 1944   85 mins (cert U)
Marvellous romantic thriller. *Gene Tierney* as the supposed murder victim with whose picture detective *Dana Andrews* falls in love.

★ **The Lawnmower Man** 1992   105 mins (cert 15)
Virtual reality makes household machines run amok in this silly, ineffectual thriller. A good idea sadly wasted – as is *Pierce Brosnan*.

★★★ **Legal Eagles** 1986   116 mins (cert PG)
Not bad mystery teams DA *Robert Redford* with lawyer *Debra Winger* and her flaky client *Darryl Hannah* on a murder trail.

★★ **The Little Drummer Girl** 1984   130 mins (cert 15)
Pretty wooden adaptation of John Le Carré's spy novel. *Diane Keaton* miscast as American girl caught up in espionage.

★★ **Lost Horizon** 1937   132 mins (cert U)
Air-crash survivor, *Ronald Colman*, discovers strange Tibetan land of love, peace and longevity in haunting Frank Capra drama.

★★ **Love at Large** 1990   97 mins (cert 15)
Thin comic thriller. PI *Tom Berenger*, hired by mysterious *Anne Archer*, discovers he's being shadowed by another PI, *Elizabeth Perkins*.

★★ **Love Crimes** 1992   85 mins (cert 18)
Disturbing thriller in which district attorney *Sean Young* is obsessed with crafty, sexy conman *Patrick Bergin*.

★★ **Mad Dog and Glory** 1993   96 mins (cert 18)
In which meek and mild police photographer *Robert De Niro* is given *Uma Thurman* by mean Mafioso *Bill Murray*, who then reneges on the deal. Disappointing considering cast. Comedy never funny, violence too heavy handed.

★★★ **Malice** 1993   111 mins (cert 18)
Alec Baldwin, *Nicole Kidman* and *Bill Pullman* in well-plotted
suspense thriller set in a New England college town, where a
brilliant surgeon, a college dean and his beautiful wife are
drawn into a web of intrigue and deception.

★★★★ **The Maltese Falcon** 1941   80 mins (cert U)
Classic, evergreen film noir/mystery from John Huston. Great
performances by *Humphrey Bogart* – as Sam Spade – *Sidney
Greenstreet*, *Peter Lorre* and *Mary Astor*. Good stuff.

★★★ **Manhattan Murder Mystery** 1994   105 mins (cert 12)
Woody Allen and *Diane Keaton* think their next door neighbour's a
killer and try to prove it, 'Rear Window' style. Co-starring
Anjelica Huston and *Alan Alda*.

★★★ **Manhunter** 1986   118 mins (cert 18)
Troubled FBI agent, *William Petersen*, must think like a serial
killer to catch one. First screen appearance of Hannibal Lecter,
played by *Brian Cox*.

★★★ **Marathon Man** 1976   126 mins (cert 18)
Absorbing thriller in which graduate student, *Dustin Hoffman*, is
unwittingly embroiled in hunt for Nazi war criminal, *Laurence
Olivier*.

★ **Miami Blues** 1990   97 mins (cert 18)
Psycho criminal, *Alec Baldwin*, and naive prostitute, *Jennifer Jason
Leigh*, doggedly pursued by victimised cop, *Fred Ward*.
Performances better than plot.

★★★★ **Missing** 1982   122 mins (cert 15)
Excellent political thriller about a father, *Jack Lemmon*, trying to
uncover mystery surrounding his son's disappearance in Chile.

★ **Mister Frost** 1990   104 mins (cert 15)
Excellent cast – *Jeff Goldblum*, *Alan Bates* – in disappointingly
stodgy Europudding in which Goldblum plays a cold-blooded
killer, convinced he's the devil.

★★ **Mona Lisa** 1986   104 mins (cert 18)
London underworld provides the backdrop for romantic thriller
with *Bob Hoskins*, *Cathy Tyson* and *Michael Caine*.

★★ **The Morning After** 1986　　　103 mins (cert 15)
Disappointing considering Sidney Lumet directs. *Jane Fonda*
wakes up next to a mysterious dead man. *Jeff Bridges* helps solve
the problem.

★★ **Mortal Thoughts** 1991　　　102 mins (cert 15)
Demi Moore and *Glenn Headley* attempt to cover up the murder of
Headley's brutish husband, *Bruce Willis*. Stylish, well-plotted but
uninvolving.

★★★ **Murder Between Friends** 1993　　　92 mins (cert 15)
Based on a true story about two men who plotted a brutal hoax and
nearly got away with murder. *Timothy Busfield* and *Stephen Lang* star.

★★ **Murder in the Heartland** 1993　　　150 mins (cert 18)
Young couple on the run and wanting to be left alone – until
they kill 11 people, that is. Stars *Brian Dennehy*, *Tim Roth* and
Randy Quaid.

★★ **Murder on the Orient Express** 1974　　　131 mins (cert PG)
Albert Finney as Hercule Poirot solving murder aboard train.
Super supporting cast all do their bit.

★★ **Narrow Margin** 1990　　　97 mins (cert 15)
Fairly tense thriller with DA *Gene Hackman* trying to protect
murder witness *Anne Archer* on perilous train trip through Rockies.

★★ **Night and the City** 1992　　　98 mins (cert 15)
Unattractive characters and dark settings do little to enhance
the appeal of a sleazy lawyer, *Robert De Niro*, moving into the
world of boxing promotion and trouble with his girlfriend's
money. *Jessica Lange* and Bob too classy for this.

★★★★ **Night of the Hunter** 1955　　　98 mins (cert PG)
Robert Mitchum as psychotic preacher on the prowl. Suspenseful
examination of good and evil. Only film Charles Laughton
directed.

★★★ **A Night to Remember** 1943　　　91 mins (cert PG)
Mystery writer and wife, *Brian Aherne* and *Loretta Young*,
investigate murder in a lively comedy/thriller.

★★ **No Mercy** 1986　　　108 mins (cert 18)
Richard Gere, a policeman bent on revenge, distracted by pouting
Kim Basinger in a violent thriller with a New Orleans setting.

★★★ **Notorious** 1946   101 mins   (cert U)
Romantic Hitchcock thriller set in Rio and involving *Cary Grant*, *Ingrid Bergman* and Nazi plots.

★★★ **No Way Out** 1987   114 mins   (cert 15)
Sex, suspense, murder and cover-up within US Government. *Kevin Costner*, *Gene Hackman* and *Sean Young* in ménage-à-trois.

★★★★ **Once Upon a Time in America** 1984   228 mins   (cert 18)
Sergio Leone's sprawling, flawed, riveting saga of Jewish gangsters in the 1920s. *Robert De Niro* and *James Woods* star.

★★★ **One False Move** 1992   105 mins   (cert 18)
Violent, engrossing thriller. Three murderous drug runners – *Cynda Williams*, *Billy Bob Thornton* and *Michael Beach* – head for town where sheriff *Bill Paxton* awaits them.

★★ **One Good Cop** 1991   105 mins   (cert 18)
Incongruous mix of sentimentality and violence. Cop *Michael Keaton* copes with dead partner's children and killers.

★★ **Out For Justice** 1991   91 mins   (cert 18)
Steven Seagal (still walking like there's something up his bottom) as a formulaic cop fighting Brooklyn baddy and old school friend. Slick, fast-paced and action-packed though totally mindless.

★ **Out of the Dark** 1988   84 mins   (cert 18)
A mysterious killer-clown strikes down girls who work for a telephone sex service. Notable, if at all, for *Divine*'s last screen appearance.

★★ **Pacific Heights** 1990   102 mins   (cert 15)
Psychological battle begins as smooth lodger *Michael Keaton* persecutes his landlords, *Melanie Griffith* and *Matthew Modine*.

★ **Paper Mask** 1990   103 mins   (cert 15)
Originally interesting, ultimately silly plot of hospital porter, *Paul McGann*, successfully posing as doctor.

★★★ **The Parallax View** 1974   102 mins   (cert 15)
Warren Beatty stars in this intriguing conspiracy theory tale, apparently inspired by John F Kennedy's assassination.

★ **Paris Trout** 1992   100 mins (cert 18)
Bigoted *Dennis Hopper* goes on a shooting spree when a black
customer refuses to pay for a second-hand car. *Barbara Hershey* is
Hopper's abused wife.

....

★★★ **Peeping Tom** 1960   109 mins (cert 18)
Once controversial Michael Powell shocker about a psychopath
who photographs his victims as he kills them.

....

★★★★ **Play Misty for Me** 1971   102 mins (cert 18)
Spurned lover *Jessica Walker* obsessively seeks revenge on DJ
Clint Eastwood. This is 'Fatal Attraction' but earlier and better.

....

★★ **The Presidio** 1988   98 mins (cert 15)
Formula thriller with soldier, *Sean Connery*, and local cop, *Mark
Harmon*, clashing during army base murder investigation.

....

★★★ **Presumed Innocent** 1990   126 mins (cert 15)
Gripping did-he, didn't-he story about an attorney, *Harrison
Ford*, as the suspect when his girlfriend is murdered.

....

★★ **Prime Suspect** 1982   100 mins (cert PG)
Adequate, made-for-TV movie in which an innocent member of
the public is persecuted after young girl's murder.

....

★★★ **The Prince of the City** 1981   67 mins (cert 18)
Treat Williams as cop who exposes corruption within New York
police force and becomes villain rather than hero. Based on
true story.

....

★★★ **Prizzi's Honour** 1985   129 mins (cert 15)
Blackly comic Mafia movie in which rival hit-persons, *Jack
Nicholson* and *Kathleen Turner*, fall in love.

....

★★★ **The Public Enemy** 1931   83 mins (cert 15)
Splendid early gangster movie – the one in which *James Cagney*
shoves a grapefruit into *Mae Clark*'s face.

....

★★ **The Public Eye** 1992   99 mins (cert 15)
Joe Pesci as 1940s photographer embroiled in Mafia murders and
threatened nightclub owner, *Barbara Hershey*.

★★ **Q & A** 1990   132 mins (cert 18)

Intelligent investigation of deep-rooted corruption within NY police force. *Nick Nolte* the bent copper; *Timothy Hutton* the crusading DA.

★ **Raising Cain** 1992   92 mins (cert 15)

Psychological thriller with *John Lithgow* as a father with split personalities who kidnaps children to experiment on them. Uneasy balance of comedy and violence.

★★ **The Real McCoy** 1993   104 mins (cert 12)

Kim Basinger as cat burglar forced into doing one last job by evil *Terence Stamp*. *Val Kilmer* is her hapless partner.

★★★ **Rear Window** 1954   112 mins (cert PG)

Hitchcock at his most stylish. Incapacitated *James Stewart* witnesses murder across the street. *Grace Kelly* helps him investigate.

★★★★ **Rebecca** 1940   130 mins (cert PG)

Daphne Du Maurier's romantic saga of young bride haunted by memory of husband's first wife directed by Hitchcock. With *Joan Fontaine* and *Laurence Olivier*.

★★ **Red Rock West** 1993   98 mins (cert 15)

Nicolas Cage and *Dennis Hopper* lead excellent cast in story of a drifter looking for work in small town and mistaken for a hired killer.

★★★ **Repulsion** 1965   104 mins (cert 18)

Roman Polanski's psychological spine-tingler depicts mental deterioration of depressed *Catherine Deneuve*, left alone in London.

★★★★ **Reservoir Dogs** 1992   105 mins (cert 18)

Not, at the time of going to press, available on video but not to be missed when it is. Quentin Tarantino's dazzling directorial debut with the story of a jewel heist that went violently wrong.

★ **Ricochet** 1992   110 mins (cert 18)

Predictable story about a psychopath hunting the man who imprisoned him. *Denzel Washington* and *John Lithgow* star.

★★ Rising Sun 1993   129 mins (cert 18)
Call-girl's murder in LA HQ of Japanese conglomerate leads to
investigation by Japanophile *Sean Connery* and cop *Wesley Snipes*.
Good, over-involved thriller which was accused of Japan-bashing.

★ The Rookie 1990   115 mins (cert 18)
Clint Eastwood as a veteran cop, *Charlie Sheen* his apprentice
partner in a feeble thriller.

★★ Ruby 1992   110 mins (cert 15)
Danny Aiello stars as Jack Ruby in British director John Mackenzie's
docudrama about the man who shot Lee Harvey Oswald.

★★ The Russia House 1990   123 mins (cert 15)
Sean Connery as London publisher embroiled in wordy, post-Cold
War Anglo–Russian espionage. *Michelle Pfeiffer* is the Moscow
love interest.

★★★ Scarface 1983   170 mins (cert 18)
Lengthy, violent remake of the old Howard Hawkes' gangster
movie, with *Al Pacino* in the Paul Muni role.

★★★★ Sea of Love 1989   113 mins (cert 18)
Scintillating, sexy thriller with *Al Pacino* investigating a series of
murders and falling for chief suspect, *Ellen Barkin*.

★★★★ Serpico 1973   130 mins (cert 18)
Al Pacino as an honest cop fighting alone against corruption in
the NYPD in Sidney Lumet's gritty, disturbing adaptation of a
true story.

★★ Shattered 1991   106 mins (cert 15)
Tom Berenger suffers from amnesia after a car crash. The plot
thickens when he hires detective *Bob Hoskins* to find out what
happened. *Greta Scacchi*, *Corbin Bernsen* and *Joanne Whalley-Kilmer*
also involved.

★★ Single White Female 1992   108 mins (cert 18)
Palm-sweating thriller of a woman's obsession with her flatmate,
spoilt by a daft ending. *Jennifer Jason Leigh* is obsessed; *Bridget
Fonda* is terrorised.

★★ **Sleeping With the Enemy** 1991   100 mins (cert 15)
Murderous husband, *Patrick Bergin*, hunting runaway wife, *Julia Roberts*, in a dreary tale. Can't see why he should want to catch her.

★★ **Sliver** 1993   115 mins (cert 18)
Thin murder mystery. *Sharon Stone* pursued by *William Baldwin* and *Tom Berenger*, one of whom is a Peeping Tom. Steamy and sexy but hugely unerotic.

★ **Society** 1989   99 mins (cert 18)
Teenage mystery, merely worth mentioning for shocking special effects – everything else is bland and dull.

★★★★ **Someone to Watch Over Me** 1987   106 mins (cert 15)
Sensational blend of romance and suspense as married cop *Tom Berenger* falls in love with the witness he's protecting, *Mimi Rogers*.

★★★ **Spellbound** 1945   111 mins (cert PG)
Hitchcock's romantic thriller wherein psychoanalyst *Ingrid Bergman* falls in love with her boss, *Gregory Peck*, while helping him prove he's not a murderer.

★★★ **Stakeout** 1987   117 mins (cert 12)
Witty thriller in which policeman *Richard Dreyfuss* falls for *Madeleine Stowe*, the woman he's meant to be watching. *Emilio Estevez* is his disapproving partner.

★★ **Stepfather** 1987   86 mins (cert 18)
Chilling performance from *Terry O'Quinn* as a man who marries widows with children in search of the perfect family, only to erupt into murderous rages when they disappoint. Followed by two inferior sequels.

★★★★ **The Sting** 1973   129 mins (cert 15)
Paul Newman and *Robert Redford* plan elaborate ruse to con crooked businessman *Robert Shaw*. Great fun but you'll need your wits about you to keep up with the plot.

★★★ **Storyville** 1992   110 mins (cert 15)
Passion, sex and political skulduggery as lawyer turned politician, *James Spader*, lands in deep trouble.

★★★ **Strangers on a Train** 1951   101 mins (cert PG)
Snappy Hitchcock direction. *Robert Walker* proposes that he and
Farley Granger should exchange murders to avoid suspicion.

★★★★ **Suspect** 1987   121 mins (cert 15)
Intriguing suspense thriller about lawyer, *Cher*, defending deaf
mute, *Liam Neeson*, on a murder charge with the illegal help of
juror, *Dennis Quaid*.

★★ **Target** 1985   118 mins (cert 15)
Average spy thriller with *Gene Hackman* and son, *Matt Dillon*,
frantically searching Paris for missing wife/mother – *Gayle
Hunnicutt*.

★★ **Teen Agent** 1991   89 mins (cert PG)
Schoolboy *Richard Grieco* is mistaken for a CIA agent while on a
school trip to Paris. No brain-stretcher but OK for the kids.

★★★ **10 Rillington Place** 1970   111 mins (cert 15)
Solid account of the John Christie/Timothy Evans murder case in
1940s. *Richard Attenborough*, *Judy Geeson* and *John Hurt* give their all.

★★★★★ **The 39 Steps** 1935   81 mins (cert U)
Cracking tale of murder, espionage and romance. Hitchcock
directs, *Robert Donat* and *Madeleine Carroll* star. A classic not to
be confused with the able, but uninspired Robert Powell
version.

★★★★ **The Thomas Crown Affair** 1968   102 mins (cert PG)
Sharp, sexy thriller featuring *Steve McQueen* as a gentleman
bank robber, *Faye Dunaway* as the insurance investigator out to
catch him and a great song – 'Windmills of Your Mind'.

★★ **Thunderheart** 1992   114 mins (cert 15)
A half-Sioux FBI man, *Val Kilmer*, is sent to a Navajo settlement
where murder and mystery abound. No big surprise at the end,
though.

★★★ **Tiger Bay** 1959   105 mins (cert 15)
A lonely girl, *Hayley Mills*, is abducted by a murderer on the run.
Sensitive story, nicely performed. Hayley's daddy, *John Mills*,
also stars.

★★★★ To Catch a Thief 1955　　　　　　　97 mins (cert U)

Fun and suspense from Hitchcock. Retired cat-burglar *Cary Grant*, suspected of robberies on the Riviera, tracks down the real culprit. *Grace Kelly* is the wealthy love interest.

....

★★★ The Trouble with Harry 1955　　　　　99 mins (cert PG)

This offbeat Hitchcock comedy/thriller about the problem of disposing of a corpse stars *John Forsyth* before his hair turned prematurely blue in 'Dynasty'.

....

★★ Turner and Hooch 1989　　　　　　　99 mins (cert PG)

Entertaining comedy/thriller concerning fastidious cop *Tom Hanks* and his slobbering dog.

....

★ Twin Peaks: Fire Walk With Me 1992　　　134 mins (cert 18)

Prequel to David Lynch's cult TV series recounting the events leading to Laura Palmer's murder. Should have been much better than it is.

....

★★ The Two Jakes 1990　　　　　　　　137 mins (cert 15)

Disappointing sequel to 'Chinatown'. *Jack Nicholson* stars and directs but still can't make the thriller thrill.

....

★ Undercover Blues 1994　　　　　　　90 mins (cert 12)

Happily married spies *Dennis Quaid* and *Kathleen Turner*, plus baby, embroiled in fatuous espionage caper.

....

★★ Unlawful Entry 1992　　　　　　　　111 mins (cert 18)

Kurt Russell and *Madeleine Stowe* terrorised by psycho policeman, *Ray Liotta*. Good idea, feebly handled.

....

★★★★ The Vanishing 1988　　　　　　　106 mins (cert 15)

George Sluizer's riveting chiller about a young Dutchman's search for his girlfriend after her kidnap in France. Mystery, tension and a truly shocking ending.

....

★★ The Vanishing 1993　　　　　　　　110 mins (cert 15)

Same story as above, same director too. But now it's set in America with *Kiefer Sutherland* as the bereaved boyfriend, *Jeff Bridges* the weird kidnapper. Hollywood takes over, tension and suspense vanish.

....

★★ Vertigo 1958　　　　　　　　　　127 mins (cert PG)

Flawed but enjoyable Hitchcock mystery with *James Stewart* as ex-cop hired to keep an eye on friend's wife, *Kim Novak*.

★★ V.I. Warshawski 1991   89 mins (cert 15)
Kathleen Turner does her best as a wise-cracking private eye but the film falls flat, thanks to a limp script.

★★ White Nights 1985   135 mins (cert PG)
Thriller starring *Gregory Hines* and Russian ballet star, *Mikhail Baryshnikov*, planning to defect from USSR to America.

★★★ White Sands 1992   101 mins (cert 15)
Pacy thriller with *Willem Dafoe* as a deputy sheriff involved with murder, money and mysterious *Mary Elizabeth Mastrantonio*.

★★★ The Wicker Man 1973   86 mins (cert 15)
Palm-sweating tale of Scottish policeman, *Edward Woodward*, investigating the disappearance of a child on an eerie island.

★★ Without a Clue 1988   107 mins (cert PG)
Sherlock Holmes send-up. Holmes, *Michael Caine*, is really a drunken actor fronting for true genius Doctor Watson, *Ben Kingsley*.

★★★★ Witness 1985   112 mins (cert 15)
Magnetic combination of action, romance, suspense and thrills. Cop *Harrison Ford* uncovers high level corruption while hiding out with murder witness in the Amish community.

★★★ Witness for the Prosecution 1957   113 mins (cert U)
Agatha Christie plot expertly adapted by Billy Wilder. Good performances by *Charles Laughton*, *Marlene Dietrich* and *Tyrone Power*.

★★ Year of the Dragon 1985   125 mins (cert 18)
Michael Cimino's violent, untidy tale of drug warfare in New York's Chinatown. *Mickey Rourke* is the investigating cop.

★ The Young Americans 1993   104 mins (cert 15)
Harvey Keitel as New York cop in London to expose drug racket. Recruits the help of local lad, *Craig Kelly*, who's reluctant to grass. Bleak but some interesting shots of London.

★ Young Soul Rebels 1991   100 mins (cert 18)
Black British drama/murder story about two DJs – one straight, the other gay – at a funky pirate radio station. Set in 1970s.

SCI-FI/FANTASY

★★ **The Abyss** 1989   140 mins   (cert 12)
'Alien' underwater but to poor effect. A group of oil rig workers
trying to rescue sunken nuclear sub. But something else lurks
in the murky depths – not suspense, that's for sure.

★★ **The Abyss: Special Edition** 1992   171 mins   (cert 12)
The director, James Cameron, saw fit to add 31 minutes to an
already overlong film. Main additions are to the special effects
which are technically brilliant.

★★★★ **Alien** 1979   117 mins   (cert 18)
Terrifying galaxy adventure of epic proportions aboard a
plagued spaceship. *Sigourney Weaver*, *Tom Skerritt* and *John Hurt*
are excellent. Fine special effects.

★★★ **Aliens** 1986   137 mins   (cert 18)
Not quite up to the original. More violence than plot but still
exciting stuff.

★★ **Alien 3** 1992   110 mins   (cert 18)
Law of diminishing returns comes in when Ripley, *Sigourney
Weaver*, is forced to confront alien again on a penal reform
planet run by *Brian Glover*, ministered to by doctor *Charles Dance*.

★★ **Alien Nation** 1988   86 mins   (cert 18)
Aliens have landed and settled in LA. *James Caan* is a police
officer investigating murder with *Mandy Patinkin* as his alien
partner.

★★★★ **Back to the Future** 1985   116 mins   (cert PG)
Michael J Fox is sent to the past to ensure his future in a terrific
movie. First and best of the series. *Christopher Lloyd* is fine as the
mad inventor of the De Lorean-based time machine.

★★ **Back to the Future Part II** 1989   107 mins   (cert PG)
Too fast, too complex, too harsh sequel has *Fox* and *Lloyd*
zipping back and forth through time like yo-yos.

★★★ **Back to the Future Part III** 1990   118 mins   (cert PG)
On form, again, *Fox* and *Lloyd* are zapped back to the wild west
where the Doc finds romance with *Mary Steenbergen*. Better than
'II', not as good as 'I' and a nice point to end the series.

★★ **Barbarella** 1968   98 mins (cert 18)
Pre-feminist *Jane Fonda* explodes onto the screen as a sexy
adventuress leched over by inhabitants of strange 41st-century
planet. Very sexy for its time, less so now.

★★★ **Batman** 1989   126 mins (cert 12)
Michael Keaton's moody hero is overshadowed by *Jack Nicholson*'s
hammy Joker. Nicholson and dark, impressive gothic sets
dominate the film.

★★★ **Batman Returns** 1992   127 mins (cert 12)
Michael Keaton still low-key as he fights such adversaries as the
Penguin *Danny DeVito*, Catwoman *Michelle Pfeiffer* and evil
entrepreneur *Christopher Walken*. Catwoman rules, OK?

★ **Batteries Not Included** 1987   106 mins (cert PG)
Aliens help poverty-stricken oldies battle to keep their home in
thin extra-terrestrial comedy.

★★★ **Blade Runner** 1982   118 mins (cert 15)
Impressive, futuristic thriller in which a cop, *Harrison Ford*,
tracks down escaped robots, *Rutger Hauer*, *Sean Young* and *Darryl
Hannah*. But wait and see . . .

★★★★ **Blade Runner: The Director's Cut** 1992   116 mins (cert 15)
Shorter and much better than the version originally released,
now that Ridley Scott has tightened things up and got rid of
that unnecessary, intrusive voice-over narration.

★★ **Body Snatchers** 1993   83 mins (cert 15)
Abel Ferrara's remake of the classic 1956 B-pic, 'Invasion of the
Bodysnatchers'. Now set on an army base in the USA but it no
longer seems to have much point.

★★ **Brazil** 1985   142 mins (cert 15)
Terry Gilliam's futuristic social satire with *Robert De Niro*,
Jonathan Pryce and Bob Hoskins achieved cult status in America.
Brilliant – but only in parts.

★★★★ **Close Encounters of the Third Kind** 1977   135 mins (cert PG)
Fantastic, thought-provoking Steven Spielberg sci-fi about
non-threatening aliens landing in America. Great special effects.

★★★ **The Dark Star** 1974   84 mins (cert PG)
John Carpenter's very inventive film about a group of slobs
cruising space and blowing up obsolete planets. This was
Carpenter's first feature.

★★ **Dark Universe** 1993   87 mins (cert 15)
Emilio Estevez stars in a melodrama about an alien-infected
spaceship that can't reach earth. A billionaire decides to launch
his own rescuing space shuttle.

★★ **Dune** 1984   131 mins (cert 15)
David Lynch's attempt to bring Frank Herbert's fantasy of a
futuristic galactic empire to the screen was reckoned a failure
in its time but it's still a bold attempt.

★★★★ **The Empire Strikes Back** 1980   124 mins (cert U)
Great action-packed sequel to 'Star Wars', reuniting cast and
crew with added special effects.

★★★★★ **E.T. The Extra Terrestrial** 1982   115 mins (cert U)
The greatest fantasy movie ever about a little boy and his
friendship with a stranded alien. Spielberg's direction plus story
and acting are quite superb. Second only to 'Jurassic Park' in
box-office takings.

★★★ **Fantastic Voyage** 1966   100 mins (cert U)
Shrunken *Raquel Welch* is injected into ailing doctor's
bloodstream to save his life. Preposterous but quite thrilling
sci-fi adventure.

★★ **Fire in the Sky** 1992   107 mins (cert 15)
Allegedy true story of a lumberjack who is abducted by aliens.
D B Sweeney and *James Garner* lend scant credibility to a drama
otherwise impossible to believe.

★★ **Flash Gordon** 1980   115 mins (cert PG)
Comic strip hero brought to life by *Sam J Jones* in lavish sci-fi
adventure. Good designs, score and supporting cast.

★★★★ **Forbidden Planet** 1956   98 mins (cert U)
Classic sci-fi version of 'The Tempest' with *Leslie Nielsen* as the
commander of a spaceship arriving at a remote, almost
deserted, planet.

★★★★ **Ghostbusters** 1984   107 mins (cert PG)
Who you gonna call if plagued by ghosts? *Dan Aykroyd*, *Harold Ramis* and the wonderful *Bill Murray*. Rib-tickling comedy with scary special effects.

★★★ **Ghostbusters II** 1989   108 mins (cert PG)
Old gang return with fewer laughs, more violence as they battle a New Year's Eve explosion of spirits.

★★★ **Highlander** 1986   116 mins (cert 15)
Action/adventure pairing of immortal 16th-century *Sean Connery* and modern day pupil *Christopher Lambert*. Enjoyable fantasy hokum.

★ **Highlander II – The Quickening** 1990   100 mins (cert 12)
Confused sequel quite unworthy of *Christopher Lambert* and *Virginia Madsen*. One can only wonder what huge amounts of money prompted *Sean Connery* to star again.

★★★ **Iceman** 1984   99 mins (cert 15)
Prehistoric man is alive and well and living in Antarctica where he's discovered by *Timothy Hutton*. Quite intriguing piece of sci-fi.

★★★ **Innerspace** 1987   120 mins (cert PG)
Astronaut, *Dennis Quaid*, is miniaturized and accidentally injected into body of hypochondriac, *Martin Short*. Fast and funny. Quaid and wife *Meg Ryan* fell in love on the set of this film.

★★★★ **Invasion of the Bodysnatchers** 1956   80 mins (cert PG)
Don Siegel's highly effective sci-fi story of unfriendly aliens taking over bodies of town's inhabitants. Seen at the time as a grim warning against Communist infiltration.

★★★ **Invasion of the Bodysnatchers** 1978   115 mins (cert 15)
Philip Kaufman's update of the original tale, now set in San Francisco and starring *Donald Sutherland*. Still very effective but loses something in the absence of the old Red scare.

★★ **Mindwarp** 1993   96 mins (cert 18)
Post-apocalyptic science fantasy – toxic zones, mutant cannibals, religious nutters and a rebellious girl, *Marta Alicia*. *Bruce Campbell* stars.

★★ **Paperhouse** 1988   94 mins (cert 15)
Engaging psychological study of pre-pubescent who enters
imaginary world of her own drawings.

....

★★★ **The Philadelphia Experiment** 1984   101 mins (cert PG)
Engaging science fiction adventure in which two US sailors,
Michael Pare and *Bobby Di Cicco*, slip through a time warp and are
transported from WWII to modern times.

....

★★★★ **Return of the Jedi** 1983   133 mins (cert PG)
Final part of 'Star Wars' trilogy, with Luke Skywalker and co up
against giant Deathstar. Special effects great as ever.

....

★★ **Return of the Swamp Thing** 1989   88 mins (cert 12)
Vegetable superhero rescues distressed damsel, *Heather Locklear*,
from evil *Louis Jourdan*. Cheap and rather cheerful.

....

★★ **Rollerball** 1975   129 mins (cert 15)
James Caan as the star of an ultra-violent sport in a futuristic
society where all other violence is banned.

....

★★ **The Running Man** 1987   103 mins (cert 18)
Imaginative, futuristic thriller in which a TV quiz show is a
matter of survival. *Arnold Schwarzenegger* is the contestant
battling for life.

....

★★★ **Short Circuit** 1986   98 mins (cert PG)
A cutesy robot comes to life to the surprise of its creator, *Steve
Guttenberg*. Acceptable sci-fi comedy.

....

★★ **Short Circuit 2** 1988   106 mins (cert PG)
Agreeable sequel, this time with the robot hitting the streets of
New York for some 'urban input'.

....

★★★ **Starman** 1984   115 mins (cert PG)
Jeff Bridges is the appealing alien, *Karen Allen* the widow who
helps him elude the police and the army to get him back to his
own planet.

....

★★ **Star Trek: The Motion Picture** 1979   132 mins (cert U)
Disappointing film version of the marvellous TV series. The
Starship Enterprise crew battle to save earth from threatening
force field. 'Star Trek II', 'III' and 'V' not up to much either.
But . . .

★★★ **Star Trek IV: The Voyage Home** 1986   119 mins (cert PG)
. . . is much more fun and contains a strong ecological message as the Enterprise lands on 20th-century Earth to save the whale. And . . .

★★★★ **Star Trek VI: The Undiscovered Country** 1991   110 mins (cert PG)
. . . is better still, though in this, supposedly the last episode, the crew are now so old that what they really need is an intergalactic zimmerframe. Still, this is the most enjoyable adventure of Kirk and company.

★★★★ **Star Wars** 1977   121 mins (cert U)
Marvellous sci-fi adventure. *Mark Hamill*, *Harrison Ford*, *Carrie Fisher*, *Alec Guinness* and robots, R2D2 and C-3PO, in hugely imaginative space-age Western.

★★ **Stay Tuned** 1992   89 mins (cert PG)
Couch potatoes *John Ritter* and *Pam Dawber* must survive 24 hours appearing on Hellvision if they're to be returned home alive. Some good spoofs and numerous throw-away lines.

★★★ **Superman** 1978   142 mins (cert PG)
Much as you'd expect. *Christopher Reeve* as Superman, *Margot Kidder* as Lois Lane and such assorted villains as *Gene Hackman*, *Terence Stamp* and *Richard Pryor* in the quartet.

★★★ **Superman II** 1980   127 mins (cert PG)
Richard Lester takes over the direction from Richard Donner and adds more visual flair to this tale in which Superman loses his powers and falls in love with Lois Lane.

★★ **Superman III** 1983   125 mins (cert PG)
Getting a bit silly now. The new villain is *Robert Vaughn*, the new lady is *Annette O'Toole* and *Richard Pryor* is woefully wasted.

★ **Superman IV: The Quest for Peace** 1987   89 mins (cert PG)
Forget it. *Christopher Reeve* co-wrote this earnest story about Superman tackling the nuclear menace. Most of the fun has gone, despite the return of *Gene Hackman*.

★★★★ **The Terminator** 1984   108 mins (cert 18)
Android *Arnold Schwarzenegger* sent back from the future to stop *Sarah Hamilton* giving birth to the future saviour of mankind. Special effects are the real stars.

★★★ **Terminator 2** 1991   136 mins (cert 15)
Arnie's back – this time as a goody protecting *Hamilton* and her son from evil Cyborg. Story takes back seat to special effects even better than in the original.

....

★★★ **They Live** 1988   94 mins (cert 18)
John Carpenter sci-fi chiller about aliens taking over Earth – and only *Roddy Piper* and his friends can see them.

....

★★★ **Timescape** 1991   90 mins (cert 15)
Small-town America is visited by a group from the future. To avert doom, widower *Jeff Daniels* has to interfere with the fabric of time itself.

....

★★★ **Total Recall** 1990   109 mins (cert 18)
Arnold Schwarzenegger provides the brawn, special effects the brain, in violent futuristic thriller in which technology can inject memories into minds.

....

★★ **The Toxic Avenger** 1985   76 mins (cert 18)
Soufflé-light spoof on comic strip heroes. A wimpy janitor falls into a tub of nuclear waste and emerges both toxic and crusading.

....

★★ **The Toxic Avenger Part II** 1989   95 mins (cert 18)
Same sort of thing – only this time Toxic is up against an evil Japanese conglomerate.

....

★ **The Toxic Avenger Part III** 1989   89 mins (cert 18)
And more or less the same again but too slapdash, too hurriedly made.

....

★★★★★ **2001: A Space Odyssey** 1968   160 mins (cert U)
Stanley Kubrick's ground-breaking account of a space journey, jeopardized when the computer takes control. Best seen in the cinema, though.

....

★★★ **2010: The Year We Make Contact** 1984   112 mins (cert PG)
Good sequel, this time directed by Peter Hyams, with a multi-national group of astronauts trying to discover what happened to the space mission of '2001'.

★★★ **Universal Soldier** 1991   103 mins (cert 18)
Dolph Lundgren the baddie, *Jean-Claude Van Damme* the good guy,
battle it out as state-of-the-art soldiers in surprisingly good
futuristic thriller. Similar to 'The Terminator' in look and
action.

★★ **The War of the Worlds** 1953   85 mins (cert PG)
Martians invade Earth. *Gene Barry* and *Les Tremayne* star in
commendable version of H G Wells story. Oscar-winning
special effects.

★★★ **Westworld** 1973   89 mins (cert PG)
Ambitious thriller set in a future where a Disneyland for adults
is staffed by robots, one of which looks just like *Yul Brynner*.

★★ **When Worlds Collide** 1951   82 mins (cert U)
Corny, end-of-the-world fable, distinguished by Oscar-winning
special effects.

★★★ **Zardoz** 1974   105 mins (cert 15)
Sean Connery and *Charlotte Rampling* in futuristic tale of
civilisation in a state of post-cataclysm. The visuals are better
than the plot.

WESTERNS

★★ **The Alamo** 1960   154 mins (cert PG)
John Wayne's long, earnest version of America's Dunkirk-like defeat in the old west. Also stars *Richard Widmark* and *Laurence Harvey*.

★★★★ **The Big Country** 1958   165 mins (cert PG)
Pleasing direction by William Wyler of a sweeping, overlong Western. Seafaring man *Gregory Peck* comes ashore to be shown country ways (and dirty tricks) by the likes of *Jean Simmons*, *Charlton Heston* and *Burl Ives*.

★★★★★ **Butch Cassidy and the Sundance Kid** 1969   110 mins (cert PG)
Unbeatable romantic, funny, action Western. Inspired pairing of *Paul Newman* and *Robert Redford* as lawless buddies.

★★★ **Cat Ballou** 1965   96 mins (cert PG)
Highly engaging spoof Western. *Jane Fonda* as school teacher turned outlaw; *Lee Marvin* a glorious drunken gunfighter.

★★ **Cheyenne Autumn** 1964   170 mins (cert U)
John Ford's last, oddly pessimistic, account of Cheyenne tribe's journey back to original settlement. *Richard Widmark* heads excellent cast.

★★ **The Cowboys** 1972   128 mins (cert PG)
John Wayne forced to take group of young boys on cattle drive and thereby help them grow up – in slow, earnest story.

★★★★ **Dances with Wolves** 1990   179 mins (cert 12)
Oscar-winning directorial debut by star *Kevin Costner* – in post-Civil War epic. Near-4hr version also available and equally worth seeing.

★★★ **Duel in the Sun** 1946   125 mins (cert PG)
King Vidor Western with *Gregory Peck* and *Joseph Cotten* fighting over half-breed, *Jennifer Jones*. Sometimes known as 'Lust in the Dust'.

★★★ **A Fistful of Dollars** 1964   100 mins (cert 15)
'Man with no name' *Clint Eastwood* blows into oldest town torn apart by feud. First and best of Sergio Leone's spaghetti Westerns.

★★★ **For a Few Dollars More** 1965   130 mins (cert 15)
Bounty hunters, *Lee Van Cleef* and the laconic *Clint Eastwood*, in
violent sequel to 'A Fistful of Dollars'. Plenty of shootouts.

★★ **Fort Apache** 1948   128 mins (cert U)
Unusual John Ford Western – an action/drama revolving
around conflict between martinet cavalry officer, *Henry Fonda*,
and pragmatic subordinate, *John Wayne*.

★★★★ **The Good, the Bad and the Ugly** 1967   180 mins (cert 18)
Clint Eastwood, 'The Good' of the title, *Lee Van Cleef* 'The Bad'
and *Eli Wallach* 'The Ugly' in top-rate spaghetti Western.

★★★★ **High Noon** 1952   85 mins (cert U)
Classic adventure with *Gary Cooper*, the sheriff, single-handedly
facing the vengeful bad guys on Main Street. Unmissable stuff.

★★★ **High Plains Drifter** 1973   105 mins (cert 18)
Mystical Western with *Clint Eastwood* as an avenging angel
cleaning up a corrupt town.

★★★ **How the West Was Won** 1962   165 mins (cert PG)
Spectacular saga covering three generations. Narrated by
Spencer Tracy and starring hordes of the great screen cowboys –
Wayne, *Peck*, *Stewart*, *Fonda*, *Widmark*, etc.

★★★ **Jesse James** 1939   103 mins (cert U)
Colourful, romanticized version of life of the notorious outlaw.
Tyrone Power as Jesse, *Henry Fonda* as brother Frank.

★★ **The Left-Handed Gun** 1958   102 mins (cert PG)
First method Western. Psychological study of exploits of Billy
the Kid, nicely played by *Paul Newman*.

★★★★ **Little Big Man** 1970   150 mins (cert 15)
Epic, imaginative saga focusing upon the reminiscences of a
120-year-old half-breed, *Dustin Hoffman*, who – among other
things – survived the battle of Little Big Horn.

★★★★★ **The Magnificent Seven** 1960   138 mins (cert PG)
Smashing adaptation of Kurosawa's 'The Seven Samurai'.
Hired guns protect Mexican village from gang of bandits. Stars
Yul Brynner, *Steve McQueen*, *Charles Bronson*, et al. Excellent.

★★ **Major Dundee** 1965   134 mins (cert 18)
Sam Peckinpah directed this disturbing, uneven drama about confederate pioneers sent to quell the Apaches. Much messed about by Columbia. *Charlton Heston* and *Richard Harris* star.

★★★ **A Man Called Horse** 1970   114 mins (cert 15)
Gory but gripping study of Sioux culture. Captured *Richard Harris* undergoes torture to prove manhood.

★★★★ **The Man from Laramie** 1955   104 mins (cert U)
Absorbing *James Stewart* Western sees him out for revenge when his brother is murdered.

★★★★ **Once Upon a Time in the West** 1968   165 mins (cert 15)
Sergio Leone's testament to the wild west, with *Henry Fonda* cast (unusually) as cold-blooded killer.

★★★ **One-Eyed Jacks** 1961   141 mins (cert 15)
Outlaw *Marlon Brando* seeks revenge on double-crossing partner, *Karl Malden*. Moody atmosphere; good direction by Brando.

★★ **The Outlaw** 1943   126 mins (cert U)
Once notoriously sexy, now tame Western. *Jane Russell* almost falling out of her bra (specially made for her) during a tumble in the hay with Billy the Kid.

★★★★ **The Outlaw Josey Wales** 1976   135 mins (cert 18)
Great Western from *Clint Eastwood* as a family man turned vigilante when wife and kids are murdered by Union soldiers.

★★ **Paint Your Wagon** 1969   166 mins (cert PG)
Nice looking musical Western. *Lee Marvin* and *Clint Eastwood* buy the same wife – *Jean Seberg* – at auction.

★★ **Pale Rider** 1985   115 mins (cert 15)
Enigmatic, slightly pretentious Western. *Clint Eastwood* as a mysterious stranger helping miners in their struggle against a large corporation.

★★ **Posse** 1993   109 mins (cert 15)
An earnest black Western, heavy on the clichés. *Mario Van Peebles* and friends chased across the west by mad colonel *Billy Zane*.

★★★★ **Red River** 1948   133 mins (cert U)

Epic movie by Howard Hawkes. A cattle drive sparks conflict between leader, *John Wayne*, and rebel, *Montgomery Clift*.

....

★★★ **Rio Bravo** 1959   141 mins (cert PG)

Enjoyable Howard Hawkes Western in which an ill-assorted quartet of lawmen, hired guns and drunks – led by *John Wayne* – fight off the bad guys.

....

★★★ **Rio Grande** 1950   105 mins (cert U)

Last of John Ford's splendid cavalry trilogy. *John Wayne* licks new cavalry recruits – one of them his son – into shape in post-Civil War era.

....

★★★★★ **The Searchers** 1956   119 mins (cert U)

The finest of all Westerns. Racist *John Wayne* seeks his niece *Natalie Wood*, kidnapped by marauding Indians, in order to kill her. *Jeffrey Hunter* wants to save her.

....

★★★★★ **Shane** 1953   118 mins (cert U)

One of the classic Westerns. *Alan Ladd*'s arrival disturbs the lives of the homesteaders he's come to protect. *Jack Palance* is marvellous as the chief heavy.

....

★★★★ **She Wore a Yellow Ribbon** 1949   103 mins (cert U)

Lavish, satisfying homage from the master, John Ford. Stars *John Wayne* as the cavalry officer reluctant to retire while the Apaches are on the war-path.

....

★★★ **The Shootist** 1976   99 mins (cert PG)

Touching performance by *John Wayne* as a dying gunfighter looking for a place to lay his holster. *James Stewart* and *Lauren Bacall* also feature. Deeply nostalgic.

....

★★★ **Silverado** 1985   133 mins (cert PG)

Not at all a bad Western with *Kevin Kline*, *Kevin Costner* and *John Cleese* heading a cast that sometimes looks uncomfortable in the old west.

....

★★★★★ **Stagecoach** 1939   99 mins (cert U)

The first great Western from John Ford with *John Wayne* as the Ringo Kid and *Claire Trevor* the tart-with-a-heart, aboard a stagecoach threatened by Red Indians.

★★★★ **Support Your Local Sheriff** 1969   93 mins (cert PG)
Charming parody pits reluctant sheriff, *James Garner*, against a
lawless mining town, as he drifts through on his way to
Australia.

★★★ **They Died With Their Boots On** 1941   140 mins (cert U)
Hollywood's lavish, whitewashed version of the Little Big Horn
battle with *Errol Flynn* as Colonel Custer, *Olivia de Havilland* his
worried wife.

★★★ **True Grit** 1969   128 mins (cert U)
John Wayne's only Oscar-winning performance as a crusty old
marshal helping a young girl, *Kim Darby*, get revenge for her
father's death.

★★★★★ **Unforgiven** 1992   131 mins (cert 15)
Clint Eastwood's marvellous, revisionist Western with superb
performances from Eastwood, *Morgan Freeman* and *Gene
Hackman*. Terrific atmosphere.

★★★★★ **The Wild Bunch** 1969   144 mins (cert 18)
Violent, riveting Sam Peckinpah Western set in 1914, when the
few remaining outlaws find the rules have changed.

★★★★ **Winchester '73** 1950   92 mins (cert U)
Fine, intelligent example of the Western genre. *James Stewart*
tracks his stolen gun across the prairies.

★★★ **Young Guns** 1988   107 mins (cert 18)
Brat Pack Western explores the romantic myth surrounding
Billy the Kid. *Keifer Sutherland*, *Charlie Sheen* and *Emilio Estevez* –
as Billy – are the young outlaws.

★★ **Young Guns II** 1990   104 mins (cert 12)
Pretty fair sequel to the above. *Christian Slater* joins cast; *Charlie
Sheen* leaves it. Rest of team remains the same.

INDEX

182